Praise for *10 ____*

"A practical bible to keep small-business owners on solid financial ground."

–Dr. Alicia Bucko, president,
Academic Dermatology Associates

"Marguerite Kirk covers in considerable depth a wide range of details in the conception of a small business, ranging from the initial planning, financial strategies, organizational tactics, to the emotional attachments involved. The book demonstrates the awesome extent and specialty of her knowledge. It shows her enthusiastic concern with issues critical to success. She powerfully argues that entrepreneurs need to learn from the past to recognize the future. As a small-business owner, I can truly say that this book is indispensable."

–Bijan Youssefzadeh, owner,
Prime Valley Beverage

"I consider *10 Commandments of Small-Business Success* my present training guide for business. The book is the basis of ... the foundation of any successful enterprise."

–Ed Pariso, owner,
Tru-Fit Equipment and Supply Co.

"A clever, entertaining and useful primer for anyone starting a business. This is a quick read and a valuable resource."

–Judy Woodruff, anchor, CNN

"Success for most Americans still lies with small business. Marguerite Kirk gives us a valuable roadmap and the tools necessary for achieving small-business success. This book is essential reading for any entrepreneur."

–Pierre Howard, two-term Lt. Gov.,
State of Georgia

"What a practical, down-to-earth, easy-to-use, straightforward, and honest success book. What's more, it's a fun, easy read, full of potent tools anyone can use to get a small business going. Best of all, it's not one of those pie-in-the-sky gloss-overs. Kirk's book presents a great understanding of how to avoid the hidden traps and pitfalls that ensnare so many. Kirk also includes a fine understanding of what most business books miss: the make-you-or-break-you human factors crucial to real success. The examples, worksheets, exercises and the step-by-step approach earn this little volume an A+ for anyone wanting the real scoop on how to effectively get a small business going."

–Dr. J. Richard Cookerly, relationship therapist,
success coach, and author, *Recovering Love*

"After reading Ms. Kirk's book ... I strongly recommend it as a must read to entrepreneurs and business owners. Ms. Kirk provides a thorough, step-by-step blueprint to building a rock-solid foundation for small- to mid-sized companies, complete with instructions on how to improve, protect and strengthen existing businesses. As an entrepreneur and professional investor, it is imperative that the companies I invest in be well grounded, and directed by adroit managers. Ms. Kirk's book outlines the foundations which allow small- and mid-sized businesses and their management to achieve the levels of success attractive to investors."

–Paul H. Adkins III, vice president,
Stellar Investments LLC

"*10 Commandments of Small-Business Success* is an easily readable, thorough primer for not only the budding entrepreneur but the existing business owner who wants to avoid the pitfalls while realizing his or her dreams. The chapter entitled 'Comply With Tax Laws: Render Unto Caesar!' is worth the purchase price of the entire book. Tax laws and procedures, which present a treacherous trap for the small-business owner, are explained in easy-to-understand language, and the dangers of carelessness and noncompliance are vividly portrayed. Worksheets for the reader's personal assessment, and analysis provided after each chapter, reveal insights that could only have been drawn from author Marguerite Kirk's real-life experiences with clients."

–Rosalie Hamilton, marketing consultant

"Marguerite Kirk delivers an educated guide and valuable strategies for establishing a successful and professional business. It is an easy guide for anyone to follow."

–Kirk and Samm Stroud, owners,
Stroud's Fitness

"Owning a small business is both immensely satisfying and challenging. Any entrepreneur should surround himself or herself with the best and brightest team, have a definable goal, be innovative, and have a copy of Marguerite Kirk's book, *10 Commandments of Small-Business Success.* The principals Ms. Kirk outlines in her powerful book are insightful and absolutely foundational to a successful business. Read them, heed them, and then have fun enjoying your success."

–Cindy Brinker Simmons, president,
Brinker Communications Inc.

"Just another book about starting a business? It is that, but much, much more. Marguerite Kirk, attorney, author and entrepreneur, has given us an imaginative, creative and practical guide for the small-business owner. Whether you are merely considering such an enterprise or regard yourself as a neophyte small-business entrepreneur, this book is for you. Ms. Kirk enumerates the pitfalls to avoid, and the positive steps to take in order to achieve success. Not only is this book extremely useable, it is quite readable. Critically placed throughout the book are worksheets to assist the reader in considering all options before action is taken. What is unique about this book is Ms. Kirk's ability to combine her knowledge of the law, her entrepreneurial skills and the psychology in achieving success into a succinct whole. A small-business owner myself, this book validated correct choices made and actions taken. At the same time, it indicated areas requiring greater focus to ensure a successful business venture. If you are embarking or have recently embarked on such an enterprise, *10 Commandments of Small-Business Success* is a must read. "

–John K. Broussard, Ed.D., licensed psychologist, and licensed marriage and family therapist

10 Commandments

of

Small-Business

Success

Marguerite Kirk, J.D.

Published by:
Bookhome Publishing
P.O. Box 5900
Navarre, FL 32566
http://www.bookhome.com

Published by:
Bookhome Publishing
P.O. Box 5900
Navarre, FL 32566
http://www.bookhome.com

Publisher's Cataloging-in-Publication
(Provided by Quality Books, Inc.)

Kirk, Marguerite M., 1944-.
 10 commandments of small-business success /
Marguerite Kirk. -- 1st ed.
 p. cm.
 Includes bibliographical references and index.
 ISBN: 1-889438-25-1

 1. Small business--Management. 2. Success in
business. 3. Entrepreneurship. I. Title. II.
Title: Ten commandments of small-business success

HD62.7.K57 1999   658.02'2
                          QBI99-84

This book is dedicated to ...

... my sons Diamond and Kai, who encouraged, assisted and believed in me all the way ...

... and the late Henry Seals of Ft. Worth, Texas, the entrepreneur whose ethics, beliefs and business practices embody all the principles of The Ten Commandments given by God to Moses, and all the rules set out in this book.

Contents

"Being good in business is the most fascinating kind of art."
–Andy Warhol

Disclaimer

This book is designed to provide information in regard to the subject matter covered. It is sold with the understanding that the publisher and author are not engaged in rendering legal, accounting or other professional services. If assistance in these areas is required, the services of a competent professional should be sought.

It is not the purpose of this book to reprint all the information that is otherwise available to the public, but to complement, amplify and supplement other texts. Readers are urged to read all the available material, learn as much as possible about running a business, and tailor the information to individual needs. Anyone who decides to run a business should expect to invest plenty of time and effort, not get rich quick.

Every effort has been made to make this book as complete and accurate as possible. However, there may be mistakes, both typographical and in content. Therefore, this book should be used only as a general guide and not as the sole source of business information.

The individuals and businesses named in this book are to provide insight into the business life. They might not endorse any or all aspects of this book, nor should their mention constitute endorsements of their products and services.

The purpose of this book is to educate, inspire and entertain. The author and Bookhome Publishing shall have neither liability nor responsibility to any person or entity with respect to any loss or damage caused, or alleged to be caused, directly or indirectly, by the information contained in this book.

If you do not wish to be bound by the above, you may return this book to the publisher for a full refund.

Acknowledgments

I owe my deepest gratitude to all the entrepreneurs who shared their special business experiences with me and helped me formulate this book:

Alicia Bucko, M.D., president of the Academic Dermatology Associates and a successful entrepreneur in her own practice in Albuquerque, N.M.; Cindy Brinker Simmons, president of her own public relations firm in Dallas, Brinker Communications Inc.; Pierre Howard, former Lt. Gov. of Georgia, a true friend and fellow attorney; Rosalie Hamilton, a marketing consultant from Dallas; LoLis Vargas and all her family for sharing their unique business experiences in traveling as The Flying Vargases, Ringling Brothers' finest trapeze act; Suzi Daggett of Insight for her generous sharing of her experiences in teaching intuitive training to entrepreneurs; Henry Simon Jr., of Ft. Worth, Texas, a nationally acclaimed bankruptcy attorney; the late Henry Seals, one of the best bankruptcy trustees in Texas, for the wisdom and integrity he shared; Steve Bloomberg, TV personality, fitness trainer and entrepreneur, for being there; Bijan Youssefzadeh, owner of Prime Valley Beverage, for sharing his startup experience; Kirk and Samm Stroud, owners of Stroud's Fitness; Ed Pariso, owner of Tru-Fit Equipment and Supply Co.; and Paul Adkins of Hoggett Kalas Investments for reviewing my manuscript and contributing suggestions that helped tell the experience of business owners.

A special thanks to Roland Kelly, who encouraged me to write my first college text; and my friend and teacher Lucille Enix, a professor at Southern Methodist University, who always demanded excellence; and Audrey Phillips, for her tireless work in typing my drafts and correcting errors.

I especially appreciate the support of my childhood friend from our old hometown of Augusta, Georgia, Judy Woodruff, a CNN anchor and senior correspondent in Washington, D.C. She took time from her busy schedule to review my manuscript.

I am indebted to Dr. J Richard Cookerly, author and relationship coach, for his suggestions; and to John Broussard, Ph.D., for his great stories and humor. My thanks to Diane Reichelt, Ed Reichelt, M.D., and Bob Stegall, M.D., who were there when I needed them in many ways.

Special thanks to my friend, Pam Bassel, who is an excellent attorney and a talented writer, for checking my manuscript for legal correctness.

Gratitude and love to my sons Diamond and Kai, who never let me get discouraged when the words seemed not to come and who believed in me always. To Arturo Orozco, my friend who taught me to never give up on my dreams.

This project became a reality because of the enthusiastic effort of my agent, Elisabet McHugh, and the tireless work and input of my editors and publishers, Scott and Shirley Gregory of Bookhome. To you, a very special acknowledgment and heartfelt thanks.

10 Commandments of Small-Business Success

Introduction

Entrepreneurs learn their lessons in two ways: from their own trial and error, or from studying the successes and failures of others.

Which is more comfortable? To turn on some relaxing music, ease into a La-Z-Boy at the end of a satisfying day's work and read a few pages of a book that will help your business? Or to spend night after night brushing dirt off your work clothes and tending to mental scrapes from another lesson learned the hard way? Most of us prefer the first alternative.

That's why I wrote this book. Whether you are thinking of starting a business, are a newcomer to the business world or are a longtime entrepreneur, this is my promise to you: this book contains some of the best business advice you will ever get.

I have spent the last 30-plus years practicing law. Most of those years were spent helping new businesses get off to a good start, getting struggling businesses back on the path to success, and working with owners of failing businesses to either reorganize or lay their enterprises to rest.

Thousands of business owners have come to me for help. Thousands of reasons for success and failure, right?

Not at all. Every one of these stories unfolded in a different way. The characters changed. But 10 themes repeated.

What an appropriate number. The Bible gives us 10 Commandments we should keep at the forefront of our minds at all times. Life's rules in 10 sentences. But how powerful they are.

Another 10 Commandments

In the spirit of God's Commandments, I have developed the *10 Commandments of Small-Business Success*. I want you to benefit from my three decades of entrepreneurial knowledge. I want you to succeed. You need not be another bankruptcy statistic. If your business follows these 10 Commandments, it succeeds. Break even one commandment, and your chances of failure increase dramatically.

Entrepreneurs are busy people. Business owners are among the hardest-working people I've ever met. They also tend to buy books, and place them on the bookshelf. Unread. This is a book you can't afford to use as a decoration. That's why I committed to keeping its length brief and its language clear. Read it in one day. Read a chapter a day. Read a page a day. But do commit to reading it. Then reread it.

After you finish this book, write down the 10 Commandments, post them on a wall or in your planner, and review them once a day to be sure you're on track. You don't want to go astray.

I always admire new business owners who are hungry for information that will help them succeed. Unfortunately, many longtime business owners lose that hunger along the way, as they get absorbed in the day-to-day details of running an enterprise. If that's you, I make this appeal: recommit to learning. It can help your business and improve your life. It is never too late.

The Age of Opportunity

America is the land of the small-business entrepreneur. Anyone can achieve the Great American Dream of owning a business. Even with the advent of multinational companies, businesses with fewer than 100 employees remain the backbone of our economy.

With the boom in technology during the 1990s, international commerce became possible from your home. Home-based businesses alone–now into the tens of millions in the United States–have increased beyond anyone's prediction and offer unlimited opportunity for people of all ages.

The type of business you open is limited only by your assets, your borrowing power, your creativity, and your belief in yourself. Just check out the Internet–it's astounding what you can buy there: everything from Oriental buckwheat pillows to chunks of the Berlin Wall to anything touched by Elvis. Often, the simplest products and services become the most successful. With hard work, creativity and cash, you'll make it.

Or will you?

Consider this statistic from the Small Business Administration:

Of all businesses in existence in 1992, more than 25 percent did not survive until 1996.

These numbers do not necessarily indicate economic failure because, of seven businesses that shut their doors, only one leaves unpaid obligations. That takes a bit of the bite out of the numbers, but still doesn't answer the underlying question:

Why is the closure rate so high?

These businesses failed because they did not follow one or more of the *10 Commandments of Small-Business Success*.

For instance, a business owner might obey The Third Commandment (Cause Cash to Flow), yet ignore the First

(Specialize in What You Know and Love). The result: the business closes because the owner can't stand going to work. You won't believe how often I hear that reason in my office as an owner comes to grips with why his business is bankrupt.

Many parents pass the American Dream of owning a business on to their children. But, in addition to teaching the benefits of owning a business, parents also must teach their children what it takes to be successful.

Take the 5-year-old down the street who sells soft drinks for $.20 a can. Yes, she is learning to be an entrepreneur. Her parents feel they are instilling the entrepreneurial spirit, but what is she learning?

She has an investor behind her: Her mother buys the drinks at the store for $.45 each and the daughter sells them for $.20. The daughter is happy in her ignorance, and her mother is proud of her enterprise. What will happen to this girl when she grows up and starts a business? If she is to succeed, she must learn The Third Commandment (Cause Cash to Flow).

Opportunity Cost

In business magazines, you will see advertisements for hundreds, even thousands of business opportunities. Most ads appeal to our emotions. While many are legitimate, far too many ads guarantee success and happiness, often claiming you can make $100,000 a year at home, working part time, with little investment and no overhead costs. They describe businesses as requiring a minimal commitment of time or money. Just sleep in, eat snack chips and watch TV while the checks roll in.

These ads repeat for one reason only: they are successful. Some people devour these business opportunities like bowlfuls of Doritos. At best, these people are in for repeated disappointment. At worst, they are risking their savings, their credit ratings and their credibility.

Consider the case of Leon:

Leon, 65, went to a free seminar on how to own a home business. He left having spent all his savings on 65 gumball machines, which were sold at the seminar. On the drive home, he was already counting his profits. All he had to do was fill the machines with gum, and go back each week to replenish the gum and collect bushel baskets of quarters. He would be rich! After all, several people in the seminar testified they now owned yachts and jets thanks to this business.

With his savings gone, Leon excitedly and optimistically bought replacement gum and charged it to his credit cards. This was better than Vegas, he thought. He sat back to wait for his jackpot of quarters.

But on his first trip to collect the profits, reality hit.

Some machines were stolen. Others were vandalized, or broken by angry customers who had lost their quarters. Leon had no idea how to repair the machines, no money to hire someone else to do it, and no insurance on the stolen ones. His dream burst like a gum bubble. He ended up with a debt he could not repay. He lost his gum machines, his savings and, most important, his self-esteem.

If Leon had known the First and Fifth Commandments (Specialize in What You Know and Love, Expect the Unexpected), he would still be collecting quarters.

Get Ready for Rain

You cannot succeed in business by believing what you see in advertisements. Watching TV late at night, you will see ads on how to make a million dollars by listening to tapes. Usually, the million dollars came from selling the tapes.

"I made $800,000 this year at home in my spare time without an investment!" one ad shouts. "I now have this beautiful California beach home complete with pool, these beautiful girls and a Mercedes, just by buying repossessed homes."

"I invested only $5,000," another program pitch man claims.

In my practice, I have had to help many opportunity seekers through bankruptcy because they bought repossessed homes and got in over their heads. The tapes might tell you how to buy the properties, but they don't tell you what to do when you own them and it rains trouble. They don't give your business an umbrella. How do you pay the mortgage if your tenants move out or must be evicted? What do you do if the economy fails, and you can't sell your properties? These realistic business situations are not taken into account on TV or in the opportunity programs, because they aren't part of the dream.

How many times have we been caught in the middle of a rainstorm while all four of our umbrellas were dry, resting side by side in the foyer closet? Let's face it–no one wants to plan ahead and get that umbrella when the sun is out. But if your business is to succeed, you need to keep your umbrella handy. You've got to be ready for when the sun ducks behind the clouds and the unexpected storm comes. And it will come.

Business owners must see beyond the magic and understand the practical message–the one we all ignored–in Cinderella. Remember, the prince tried the glass slipper on many women before he found Cinderella. He developed a plan, and put together a practical approach that worked. The reunion was magical and romantic, but it was the plan that got them together.

The *10 Commandments of Small-Business Success* will ensure you are looking at your enterprise in the proper light, and will give you a solid foundation to better handle entrepreneurial challenges. Should the inevitable rain turn to a storm, I have included a Financial First Aid Kit at the book's conclusion that will help you assess your situation and make wise decisions about what to do from there.

Start today to learn and apply the *10 Commandments of Small-Business Success.*

It's easy to remember them: just think of the word "successful":

Specialize in What You Know and Love
Understand the Entrepreneurial Mindset
Cause Cash to Flow: Create a Sound Business Plan
Comply with Tax Laws: Render Unto Caesar!
Expect the Unexpected: Learn to Recognize Problems
Seize Prosperity
Seek Silence in Chaos
Form a Firm Foundation
Use Professional Advisers
Learn To Turn Coal into Gold

In the next 10 chapters, I will tell you in simple language how to realize your dream, whether your business is local or extends throughout the world.

Remember, these are commandments–not options. If you are missing even one letter of SUCCESSFUL, you are headed for trouble.

Make your business a lasting success!

A Stormy Tale

One blustery spring day, I stopped at a neighborhood convenience store for gasoline and a soft drink. The store was full of groceries, empty of customers, and the cashier chattered constantly.

I asked him, "Do you own this store?"

"Yes," the newly naturalized American citizen responded, "I do, but the bank may own it soon if this rain continues. I'm in a good place here by the lake. There are no other markets nearby; I even sell fish bait. But, this year and last, the rains have ruined my business. No one wants to go to the lake in the rain. I don't know how long I can stay open under these conditions. I came to America to find my dream, and I found out that it rains here, too."

He said it all when he said, "It rains here, too." It rained, and he had no umbrella. He assumed the risk and went after the American Dream, but where was the profit? We can blame his business woes on the weather, but he could have made it, had he known the all-important rules described in this book.

A short time later, two more convenience stores owned by large oil companies were built nearby. A gasoline price war started. Because our hero had used all of his capital to offset the slow business caused by the rain, he could not lower his prices to compete. He could not restock his inventory, so even the loyalists went elsewhere. Finally, he lost the store to bankruptcy.

He made mistakes in the beginning: he paid too much for the business. He bought a dream. He had no savings or credit lines, so he could not service the debt when things got rough. When he bought the store, he did not use professional advisers because he wanted to save the fees. He lacked knowledge of the market and how to compete. This was his first business venture, and he paid expensively for his lessons.

Today, in that same store, customers stream in and out, even in the rain. What happened? A family following the concepts outlined in this book bought the store at foreclosure and succeeded. They lowered gasoline prices and offered free grocery delivery. They added take-out chicken, barbecue, and picnic box lunches for the nearby lake. When you walk in to pay for the gas, the enticing smell of food cooking makes your mouth water. They have the sizzle *and* the steak. Even with the tough competition nearby, the store thrives because it is unique.

What made the difference? In this case, the second owner knew how to apply The Sixth Commandment (Seize Prosperity). He reached his business dreams, and was able to send his children to excellent schools–both priorities in his life.

Follow the *10 Commandments of Small-Business Success*, and thou shalt increase your odds of victory.

To your success,
Marguerite Kirk

The First Commandment

Specialize in What You Know and Love

"Work is love made visible. And if you cannot work with love but only with distaste, it is better that you should leave your work and sit at the gate of the temple and take alms of those who work with joy."

—Kahlil Gibran, *The Prophet*

"Have a lot of kid in you. If you have fun at what you do, you'll never work a day in your life. Make work like play, and play like hell."

—Norman Brinker, *On The Brink*

Aristotle once said, "Those who wish to succeed must ask the right preliminary questions."

If you want to succeed in your business, you'll need to answer these preliminary questions:

- Will I enjoy this line of work?
- Will my business be consistent with my values?
- Do I know what I'm doing, and am I using my talents?
- Does this business fit my ideal lifestyle?

If you can answer yes to these questions, you're on your way to obeying The First Commandment: "Specialize in What You Know and Love."

Business With the Greatest of Ease

The Flying Vargas Family, a renowned trapeze group from Mexico City, is an excellent example of entrepreneurs who follow The First Commandment. As of this writing, they are touring the world with Ringling Brothers Barnum and Bailey Circus.

Generations of the Vargas family have been trapeze flyers. The leader, Alejandro Vargas, tells wonderful stories of taking the family circus throughout the jungles and villages of Mexico. They traveled in wooden wagons down dirt roads, bringing their magical show to remote areas. Villagers wielded machetes to cut paths through the thick, green jungle to allow the Vargas family, with their elephants and lions, to come in. Most villagers had never seen an elephant, much less the spellbinding family who wired trapeze cables between trees and swung free in the air while performing triple somersaults without a net.

Today, Alejandro's young son and daughter practice on the trapeze nightly; soon they will join the act. Maricela, Alejandro's sister, flies with her brother, and also designs the costumes. Alejandro's wife, LoLis, handles the business details, which include setting show dates, negotiating contracts down to the finest detail, and handling public relations. LoLis speaks of going to law school to specialize in contract and entertainment law, which would help her on the business side. With her energy, enthusiasm and drive, she would do well. But her first love is performing, and she will always return to that. The love of performing and family values keep the Vargas family together as they travel the world. The circus is their life—they specialize in what they know and love.

Water Wheels

The sun finally broke through after a week of storms, and my car was dirtier than the *Starr Report*. One successful entrepreneur was ready to work. Two men drove up to my house in a shiny red truck that read, "Mac's Mobile Car

Wash." For $15, Mac and his assistant will wash your car in your driveway, or in your company parking lot while you work.

Mac is a walking encyclopedia of car washes: He can tell you the prices at the other wash businesses in town, and how long it will take to drive there and wait. Figuring what your time costs, he calculates your savings. He can tell you, in detail, how his cleaner is better for your car's paint than his competitors' products. He knows his business, and knows what his customers want and need.

Mac started his mobile car wash when he was laid off from a 20-year job. The company he had worked for went broke, and he lost his retirement savings. Mac adapted and turned his adversity into success. He says he has the freedom to work as much as he wishes and has job security—cars always get dirty. He loves rain! I hire him to wash my cars partly because he's an inspiration, and I love to be around his enthusiasm.

Find Your Passion

If you are considering starting a business, how do you know the business is right for you? The question most people ask is, "What business can I get into and make a lot of money in?" But you probably won't make money if you don't like what you are doing and, if you do happen to turn a profit, you certainly aren't going to get the most out of life that way. Money and love of your work need not be exclusive. Ask yourself:

• If I could get into any line of work in the world, what would it be?
• What are my hobbies?
• How do I enjoy spending free time?

People are so used to the job mentality that they often push love of work to the bottom of the priority list when they think of starting a business. Don't make that mistake. You are going to spend a huge chunk of your life building a business. Spend it doing something you love, something you believe is important.

Often, a hobby can evolve into a successful business. Debbi Fields loved to bake cookies, and that led to the Mrs. Field's empire. Bill Gates played endlessly with computers, and his parents worried that nothing would come of it.

There's no better way to spend your work hours than by doing something you enjoy.

A Fitting Choice

Josh was a schoolteacher–and good one, at that. However, he was tired of the school system's problems: guns, drugs and too many teachers who were poor role models. At age 40, he had invested much of his life in something that wasn't what he wanted. What else could he do?

Josh had been lifting weights since he was 12 and had won several power-lifting contests. Exercising and weightlifting were his passions outside of the classroom. He also enjoyed giving advice to friends and helping them become physically fit.

Letting passion be his guide, he decided on a big move: he left his job and started teaching people how to be fit at a nearby gym. He knew bodybuilding better than anything, and he loved it. Using his entrepreneurial skills, he added a vitamin and supplement line to sell at the gym. Using his educational skills, he wrote a business and training manual for personal trainers.

Today, Josh is known as one of the best, most knowledge-able personal trainers in his city. To him, his business is not work.

Salad Days

A good friend of mine and his wife love to cook and experiment with new recipes. They frequently invite me over to test their new concoctions. After extensive research and planning, they decided the time was right for Fred to quit his engineering job and launch a catering company.

That little venture has since bloomed into a huge, international business that sells potato salad, chicken salad, beans and premixed gourmet salads to restaurants.

Heirs to family businesses often suffer because they violate The First Commandment. Parents often expect that, when they retire, one or more of their children will take over the family business. But while the heirs might inherit financial security, their passions might lie elsewhere. Too often, they bury their dreams to please their parents, or decide to play it safe rather than take a chance on something new.

I feel bad for the so-called "opportunity seekers" in the business world. For them, the lure of money comes above everything else, and that approach is doomed to fail. Many of these people end up trading a job they didn't like for a business they don't like either, but hope will pay off big. They choose the business because someone told them he got rich from it, and that they should hop aboard the gravy train, too. The disappointing results often kill both the enterprise and the entrepreneurial spirit in them. They violated The First Commandment.

Business needs to be about more than money.

If you are already in business, you probably know if the business is right for you. If you haven't verbalized it, you know it in your gut. Do you look forward to going to work? If not, it's a red flag that something needs to change. If your business is making a profit, but you hate going to work, you are not following The First Commandment. And, unless you can change your business so it is pleasurable for you, you aren't living life to its fullest, and you might end up closing your doors. In fact, if you know you have a passion in another field, you might want to set the wheels in motion to change businesses now.

Passion and excitement, as exemplified by the Vargas family and Mac, are the fuel any entrepreneur needs when problems arise. With these qualities, problems become challenges instead of obstacles.

True Value

Success and failure are not absolutes. You can't turn to Page 180 of this or any book, read a definition of success and say, "Yep–I've made it." An entrepreneur might earn $10 million a year, yet consider himself a failure. Another might scrape for 10 years to pay the bills, and consider himself a walking, talking business success.

Have you thought about what success and failure mean to you? If you haven't, how will you know when you get there?

What do you value most in life? Specializing in what you know and love means you align your business with your values, which are your beliefs about what is most important in life.

In *Care of the Soul*, Thomas Moore discusses the importance of choosing a profession with soul value–your work must embody the values and truths you feel at your deepest level. Tami Coyne, in *Your Life's Work*, stresses that our work is the expression of our spirit, our soul.

This idea has been around for ages. The Bible tells us to first seek the Kingdom of God, then all else will be given to us.

The entrepreneur who loves her business and feels great about her contribution to the world will put her heart and soul into it, and be successful.

Your values have evolved throughout your life, and continue to change as you grow. Your values have been affected by people in your life–your parents, classmates, friends, teachers, professional colleagues, church members and relatives. Even people you might have never met but who reached you through the media–baseball players, TV personalities, movie stars, musicians and authors–have an impact.

Being a musician doesn't cause you to drink heavily and use drugs, but many rock stars adopt not only the musical styles of their heroes, but also their troubled value systems.

On stage, there's the example of Chris Farley, who not only emulated his hero, John Belushi, as a comedian, but also lived the same drug- and food-abusing lifestyle and ended up dying the same, sad way at a young age.

One man sits in jail and remains proud that he killed hundreds of adults and children by driving a truck bomb into a federal building, while another woman went to her grave being equally proud she spent her life helping the poor in third-world countries. How can this be? It all goes back to their values.

If you value helping others, then your business should be service-oriented. If you value adventure, consider a business that will take you to exciting places. If you put a high value on security, avoid businesses such as restaurants, which are high-risk ventures. If you value face-to-face communication, open a travel agency or become a tour guide, but don't become a lighthouse attendant.

Advocating Values

Peter works as an attorney in a large firm. He yearns to be powerful and successful in his law practice. He also values time with his family. To be successful in this firm, he is required to put in long, demanding hours. As a result, he has little time for his family. Peter has to resolve his conflict by deciding which value is more important. He might be able to solve his situation by working for himself, or for a less-aggressive firm.

Your values can include: adventure, love, status, friendship, respect, authority, creativity, moral fulfillment, fun, personal growth, challenge, independence, money, variety, excitement, honesty, security.

You probably can list many others. What do you value most in life? Is your business aligned with your values?

For example, gambling has become a huge industry. But if you feel gambling is morally wrong, could you run a successful casino? No! Either your business will suffer, or the guilt will eat away at you.

Many entrepreneurs face this dilemma: their business is profitable, but they can't stand the product or service they are selling. It isn't always obvious at first. Maybe an insurance broker knows she is selling a product that can save her customers from financial ruin. That makes her feel good about her line of work. On the other hand, she can make a heck of a lot more money selling customers more insurance than they need. So, she starts making justifications to herself for overselling. Pretty soon, she dreads going to work each day.

You shouldn't have to make excuses for your line of work. In fact, you can't, over the long haul. Violating your values always catches up with you. Always.

Skills and Knowledge
for Fun and Profit

Ever wish you could hit a baseball 400 feet and cash in on one of those $100 million paydays that are growing commonplace in sports? It's a great dream, but for most of us, our baseball careers never were and never are going to happen.

We all have God-given talents that get better with experience and learning. What skills do you have that you could turn into a business? More important, which skills do you have that you enjoy using over and over again?

You might be a mathematical whiz. But if the thought of becoming an accountant and working with numbers day in and day out bores the life out of you, you'd be better off taking on a different line of work.

What talents do you have? What do people tell you that you are good at? Your talents could include things such as: reading, writing, speaking, drawing, selling, listening, problem-solving, motivating, persuading, painting, drama, fund-raising.

Your talents and expertise go beyond self-satisfaction–they will play a huge role in your business success. Have you ever been in a retail store where the employees knew little about what they were selling? Do you want to shop at a health-food store staffed with pale, flabby employees who need help lifting a two-pound jar of vitamins? Do you feel confident using the service of a beautician with dry, tangled and uneven hair? Would you buy beef from a vegetarian? Would you go back to a vegetable stand where the cashier points to your squash and asks, "Are those carrots or tomatoes?"

Imagine calling Widget World to ask about their new mini-widgets, only to be told, "I don't know anything about them." So you ask to speak to someone who can help you. The answer? "Sorry. I just bought this company and no one else is here."

Do you feel like shopping at Widget World any more?

Each small business has unique knowledge requirements. And it's amazing how many small-business owners know so little about what they sell. Entrepreneurs who want to be successful need a solid understanding of both good business principles and the ins and outs of their specific business.

Hair Apparent

Marguerite Michelle's business is entertainment and selling hair-care products. For Michelle, an acrobat, knowing her business truly is a matter of life and death. Her unique knowledge requirement: hair! She hangs from a trapeze held only by her strong, healthy hair. When she's in the shower, she doesn't grab whichever bottle of shampoo happens to be handy. Michelle has a first-hand experience of hair-care products and vitamins that keep her long, black hair the best it can be.

Don't lose your grip and plummet into a financial abyss. Knowledge will mean the life or death of your business as years go by.

You can't know everything before you open a business, but you must commit to learning something new about your business every day. Read books. Listen to tapes. Surf the Internet. Attend seminars. Use consultants. With fierce competition and today's rapidly changing marketplace, it's more vital than ever to keep up in your field. Your customers need to know that you know what you're talking about. And, with a solid foundation of knowledge, you can make informed business decisions with confidence.

Lifestyle

People often neglect to consider lifestyle considerations when deciding what type of business to run, and where they will run it.

Most people spend their lives within 100 miles of where they were born. They don't have to, but they do.

If you don't like where you are living, move somewhere else!

What would you consider the perfect place to live and work? Another city? Out in the country? A beach town? Somewhere warmer? Somewhere colder? Europe? A Caribbean island? You need to decide what type of surroundings will be best for you and your business.

Before you invest money, you also need to know what lifestyle will be required by the business you open. Thinking of becoming a bagel baker? Will you bounce out of bed at 3 a.m., start baking and be happily whistling when the first customers arrive? Or do you stay naturally groggy and grumpy until noon? Think you'll have many customers if you open the bakery late, scowl when you take orders and serve cold coffee and yesterday's bagels?

If you hate mornings, don't open a bakery. If you are allergic to grass, don't start a landscaping business.

Booking a Change

Mary's parents owned a successful public relations firm. As do many entrepreneurial parents, they wanted her to take over the business when they retired. Their business required a lot of entertaining, but Mary was more comfortable in the corner with a book. As difficult as it was for them to admit, her parents realized it was better for them to sell the business. Mary opened a used bookstore, became an expert on old books and succeeded. Her parents, meanwhile, had extra money from the business sale to enjoy their retirement.

Many would-be entrepreneurs dream of owning a restaurant. What people don't realize is that most restaurant owners leave home while their kids are in school and don't return until long after the spouse and children are in bed. And, they work weekends. It is a commitment to a demanding way of life.

What does your potential business entail? A great way to find out is to seek a job at an existing business in that field. Watch what is required of the owner. When does she come in? When does she leave? What does she do all day?

Although first-hand observation is best, if you don't want to take a job, at least go into several similar businesses and strike up conversations with the owners. Don't march in and say, "Hi. I'm thinking of opening a business just like yours across the street, and I'd like you to tell me how your business works." Just talk, customer to owner. You'd be amazed at what people will tell you if you just ask.

A Home Run?

As another lifestyle consideration, you might want to consider running your business out of your home. While the mix of work and family life certainly is not for everyone and has its share of challenges, some who run home businesses say it is the perfect way to live and work. You can chase business dreams with your spouse and kids, and spend more time with your family. But you need discipline and maturity to make a home business enjoyable, and to keep it from interfering with your home life.

Home businesses also can be an answer for single parents, retirees, people with disabilities, and anyone who wishes to try a new business without going heavily into debt.

Do plenty of homework, however, if you are considering any sort of home-based "opportunity." Many such offers are garbage that are not based in sound business principles.

The IRS has recognized the validity of a home business and allows many deductions, including portions of your mortgage payments, utilities, taxes, and other expenses necessary for the business. So, if working at home fits your lifestyle, go for it–you might end up with more profit.

If you decide to work from home, though, remember to treat your business as a business. Act like a professional and, accordingly, charge what your products or services are worth. Don't come to the door in your pajamas.

Serve Thy Customer

You're not the only one who is going to benefit if you love your line of work, align your business with your values, know your profession inside and out, and tailor your business to fit your lifestyle. Your customers will, too.

Yes, We Make Doghouse Calls

Mark has an unusual veterinary business. He operates a mobile van called Doggie Vet and Grooming Service. His service might not be vital to you when Fido needs her annual shots ... if Fido is a calm, well-behaved poodle. But if your Fido is a high-strung Great Dane who makes a great mess all over you and your car's leather upholstery every time you're halfway to the vet, it's a lifesaver. Mark has specialized in what he knows and loves, and his customers benefit from his exceptional service.

If you love what you do, you will enjoy meeting customers. If you hate your work, you will avoid them at all costs. A small-business owner cannot hide from customers and be successful. He must be available to solve problems and answer questions. Customers who choose small businesses over large franchises and chain stores do so because the owner is accessible and, if they have a problem or special request, they expect to see the boss. Even though small businesses often cannot compete on all price levels with larger conglomerates, they can excel at personal service.

All businesses sell either services or products. The owner is the image behind the sale. Her values and ethics become the company's. People often seek out attorneys, dentists or other professionals based on a reputation of giving good service at a fair price. Customers give repeat business to certain cleaners because they know any problem will be handled fairly and quickly.

Great advertising does not create a successful business unless the customer service is there to back it up.

You, as the owner, must know why your product or service is better than the competition's. You must believe in yourself, and sell your customers on you.

Customer service is about what the customer wants and needs, not what you think he should want.

A great way to find out if your service is good is to ask your customers what they think of your business. This will provide valuable feedback and allow you to stay in tune with what your customers want and expect.

One famous customer survey was done by Norman Brinker, founder of Steak & Ale, Chili's, Macaroni Grill, and other casual dining chains. Brinker would dress as a country boy, stand outside his restaurants and ask customers how they liked their meals and whether he should eat there. You can't get more service-oriented than that.

If you specialize in what you know and love, you will be excited about your work and give superior service.

Make Your Dreams Reality

Follow the example of the previous successful entrepreneurs. Fly like the Vargas family, wash like Mac, lift weights like Josh and scrub dogs like Mark–or do whatever you do with enthusiasm and exceptional service. If you have a talent and love for something, turn it into an income-producing business.

Don't just sit there and dream—explore, make it reality. If you don't, 10 years from now, as the red Mobile Car Wash truck rolls by, you will say, "I could have done that."

If you are reading this book before deciding what type of business to open, the following exercises will help you get started. If you are operating a business, the worksheets will give you new ideas about how to make changes so you will specialize in what you know and love.

Exercise One

Do this, and all exercises, on separate sheets of paper. Write down at least 10 talents and skills you have: painting portraits, working with wood, an ability to get along with people, a knack for problem-solving ... anything that comes to mind. Be sure to list all your skills, even if they don't seem practical. Also, include positive attributes other people have recognized in you. Sometimes, others see our talents before we do.

Example:

> 1. I am a good negotiator.
> 2. I play a mean game of chess.
> 3. I am a good writer.

Exercise Two

Next, list at least 10 things you like to do with your leisure time. What you prefer to do with your free time indicates possible unexplored business ventures. Hobbies tell us where our passions lie.

Example:

      1. I enjoy eating at restaurants.
      2. I love boating.

Exercise Three

Describe, in detail, the lifestyle you would like. Include where you want to live, what hours you want to work, how you like to dress, the number of people you would like to work with, etc. In an ideal situation, what would be the perfect way to spend each day?

Example:

I want to run a home business, live in a warm climate, dress casually, etc.

Exercise Four

List at least the top 15 things you value in life. Then, rank these in order of importance, with number one being the most important to you, number two the second-most important and so on. Make sure you compare all the values and put them in the right order.

Example:

      1. Self-respect
      2. Independence
      3. Creative expression
      4. Learning new things
      5. Having fun

Exercise Five

Compare the lists, and come up with four or five businesses you could run. If you already run a business, you might be able to expand your business to include more of what you enjoy. Following are just a few options. For more ideas, turn to the Yellow Pages of your telephone book and see how many types of businesses are possible!

Like being creative?

Baby clothes designer	Herb gardener
Caterer	Newsletter publisher
Gift basket creator	Picture framer
Graphic designer	Specialty food retailer

Enjoy fixing things?

Antique restorer	Doll doctor
Computer repair person	Home improvement expert

Need lots of people in your life?

Bed & breakfast operator	Public relations expert
Career counselor	Real estate agent
Child care provider	Senior daycare provider
Family history recorder	

Can't sit still?

Adventure trip planner	Fitness instructor

Enjoy parties?

Convention coordinator	Seminar producer
Party planner	Wedding planner

Like to make others happy?

Grocery shopping service owner	Plant caregiver
Personal image consultant	Resume writer
Personal shopper	Temporary agency operator
Pet sitter	

Are you the tidy type?

Auto detailer	Office cleaner
Maid service provider	

Are numbers your thing?

Bookkeeper

Business broker

College scholarship consultant

Database designer

Fund raiser

Medical claims expert

Like to work with data?

Computer instructor

Headhunter

Indexer

Information broker

Medical transcriptionist

Questionnaire designer

Technical writer

Turned on by the Information Age?

Chat moderator

Online customer service specialist

Online publisher

Web retailer

Website designer

The Second Commandment

Understand the Entrepreneurial Mindset

"No man is born into the world, whose work is not born with him."

—James Russell Howell, *A Glance Behind the Curtain*

Ads in popular business magazines boast of how easy it is to earn up to $10,000 a month in profit at home with your computer.

What the ads don't hype is that it isn't the magical opportunity that creates the five-figure profit a month; it's the ambition, work and entrepreneurial drive of the person behind the computer.

Yes, you can earn a six-figure income in a small- or home-based business. But let's get one thing clear: you will never, ever do it without good, old-fashioned hard work. There are no shortcuts, and anyone who tells you otherwise is selling you snake oil.

Do you really want to own your own business? Are you willing to work long hours? Are you a good leader and manager? Are you comfortable letting the responsibility stop with you? If your business falls into trouble–and they all do, to some degree–do you have what it takes to hang in there and fight it out? Will you sacrifice today so you can have a better life tomorrow?

In working with thousands of clients, I have found four consistent factors that influence the success or failure of a business. The great news is that, with discipline and perseverance, anyone can develop these habits for success.

Successful entrepreneurs must:

1. Be there to mind the store. They show up every day, work hard and make personal sacrifices.

2. Not give up in hard times. They persevere, even when times look bleak.

3. Avoid the "excuse book trap." They take full responsibility for their businesses, including their failures.

4. Stay flexible. They grow with the business, which allows their enterprise to adapt to changing times and lets them take calculated risks.

Who's Minding the Store? You Are!

A small business needs its owner's commitment and excitement. If you are not willing to roll up your sleeves and get down to business, day in and day out, you can rarely be successful. Let's look at four examples of business owners who are involved with their enterprises to differing degrees:

South of the Border and Out of the Way

Location is vital to the success of most restaurants, so the small, Mexican dining establishment began at a disadvantage when it opened in an out-of-the-way neighborhood shopping center. While the restaurant might not have been in Manhattan, it had something else going for it: an energetic owner. Lunch, dinner, weekdays, weekends ... every time I went in, he was there, hard at work with the rest of his family and employees.

The owner made me and his other customers feel like family. He remembered our names, struck up conversations at appropriate times, brought us samples of new menu additions and greeted our departure with a warm handshake and sincere thanks for coming in. He was proud of his restaurant and loved what he was doing.

Within five years, the business had been named among the top five Mexican restaurants in the Dallas/Ft. Worth area. When it moved to a fantastic location in a thriving shopping center and expanded, I didn't know what to expect when I walked in. Sometimes, success causes owners to disappear. But the minute we strolled in, the owner waved from across the room and rushed over to our table to welcome us. The dining experience was as wonderful as ever, thanks to the owner who was there to ensure that was true.

The Vietnamese French Baker

Anna came to the United States from Vietnam in 1989. She began her new life in America as a grown woman without a single possession. But she and her husband managed to open a small, French bakery in a shopping center after scraping together their investment money. Borrowing from relatives was the only way she could get the capital she needed–she couldn't go to the bank and borrow money because she could hardly speak English and had no collateral.

For years, Anna often worked more than 18 hours a day. Yet, she always had a smile on her face, and free cookies for the children and samples of French bread for the adults.

I asked her how she could work so much and still carry that radiant smile: "It will be worth it–you'll see," she said amid that day's wonderful smells of cherry tarts and hazelnut coffee. "My son goes to a good school. He will have what he needs. It is hard now, but I love my work and it is mine. We lost everything in Vietnam, but we will have it in America. I don't doubt that we will succeed, because I won't quit until we do."

That tiny investment of money and huge investment of time and love have produced great dividends for Anna and her family. Within seven years, the bakery was thriving, and she and her husband opened a second successful store.

Paging Dr. Smith ... Dr. Smith ... ?

A group of big-city doctors decided to band together to try to cash in on the health-food craze. They formed a corporation, coughed up big money and opened a health-food store. They took the "lazy-faire" entrepreneur's approach toward the business: "We'll put up the money, hire someone to do the work, and sit back and collect the profits."

The doctors hired a manager and gave him authority over all aspects of the business. No auditing was done. After a year, the doctors were happy with the way the business was progressing ... until the store's suppliers began calling the doctors at their offices to complain their products were not being paid for. The doctors investigated and discovered the store's bills were five months behind. When they went to confront the manager, he was gone, and had taken the funds in the store's business account with him.

At the time, the only relief available was to file a Chapter 7 bankruptcy. That eliminated the corporation's debts but did not let the doctors off the hook for their personal guarantees or the unpaid employee taxes.

Don's Construction Company

Don put in years of hard work to build a profitable construction company. Then he suffered a heart attack. So he hired a friend to take over the business while he was in the hospital and during his recovery. The friend could drive a forklift with the best of them but had no experience running a business. Six months later, the company had to file for bankruptcy. There was nothing else Don or his attorneys could do to help, as adequate books and records were not kept during Don's absence.

The last two examples show one of the primary reasons businesses fail: lack of adequate personal attention from the owner. If you are not directly involved in the small business you are investing in, chances are you are headed for failure.

The health-food store was a dream of one of the doctors. If he had been checking on the store during evenings and weekends, chances are he and his partners could have avoided bankruptcy. In the case of Don's construction company, the owner could not help being in the hospital. Unfortunately, as soon as he was absent, his business failed. What could he have done to prevent his business failure? If he had followed The Third Commandment (Cause Cash to Flow) and developed a good business plan, he would have been able to overcome his health problem's effect on his company.

A small business is an extension of you. You must be there frequently, solving problems with a smile on your face. An absentee owner–or one who's there with a bad attitude–can break a company. That doesn't mean you have to work yourself to death. You need a life away from work, and you need vacations. In fact, many business owners are guilty of overworking, and that also can take its toll on a business–and it certainly does on the owner. It's all about balance.

Be there. Your business success depends on it.

Persistence Pays

Successful owners must not give up when times are difficult. You will face plenty of moments when you throw up your hands in disgust and scream in your head, or at the top of your lungs, "That's it. I'm going back to working for someone else. I've had it." The next day, however, are you going to be at your desk trying to get your business back on track? Or will you be revising your resume?

The American Dream comes in many shapes and sizes. I have an unusual client who taught me a lesson or two about tenacity:

Mr. Roper

Mr. Roper is 78 years young, and his business assets consist of 40 acres of used, black-sided car tires. Acres and acres of rubber. To some, it's a tire graveyard. To Mr. Roper, it's an enterprise.

He has built mosquito houses, an irrigation system and a winter greenhouse out of used tires. He sells these items in his store–his weather-beaten barn. The mosquito houses are good sellers–Mr. Roper convinces his customers that if mosquitoes are happy in their own homes, they won't go roaming and bite people. He is the ultimate salesman.

While Mr. Roper certainly is a creative inventor, he is not a financial wizard. He lacks a formal education and cannot read. He did not understand the property-tax notices, so he did not pay his taxes. When he came to see me, the county was about to foreclose on his land and sell his property out from under him.

My first impression was that he must be one of those hopeless cases, because I did not know of a booming mosquito house market. I did not even know a mosquito would live in a house! But after we talked awhile, it was clear Mr. Roper had a personality that would overcome his lack of knowledge.

We were able to negotiate a payment plan with the county. That was a pleasant surprise, but the bigger thrill was watching this man make his tax payments for a full year, then sell a piece of his land to eliminate his tax debt. Mr. Roper's spirit and tenacity won over obstacles.

The last time I spoke with Mr. Roper, he was trying to get a patent on some new inventions. He told me he had invented a way to turn coal into gold. He inspired the last chapter in this book, where we will go into greater detail about tenacity.

Though his ideas are, well, unusual, Mr. Roper loves his business and did not give up when times got hard. It doesn't matter what you or I might believe–he believes in his business. If you meet Mr. Roper, I'll bet you will buy a mosquito house for your yard. I did!

Well, Excuuuusssse Me

When my son Kai was 6, I decided he would become a great piano player. Of course, he had different ideas. We struggled through lessons ... OK, I struggled, he couldn't have cared less. After six months, his excuses to the piano teacher for why he had not practiced grew more and more creative. They started with, "The dog ate my music sheets" and went downhill from there. My favorite was, "We don't have any pencils at our house."

The teacher, Mrs. Bowles, used to smile and say, "Yes, Kai, that is Excuse No. 39 in my Excuse Book. Don't you have a new one for me?"

Whenever I'm tempted to blame someone or something else, I think of Mrs. Bowles' Excuse Book. While I was paying her to teach my son, little did I know that I was the one who would learn a great lesson: accept no excuses.

Successful owners take full responsibility for their businesses and avoid making excuses–to themselves, their employees or their customers. Unexpected events happen every day: the computer system goes down, shipments don't arrive on time, shipments don't arrive at all, key employees get sick (or, at least, call in sick). Successful owners welcome challenges, and see these as opportunities to be creative.

Most clients and customers don't expect everything to be perfect. But they do want to believe the business owner is working to solve problems rather than hide behind excuses.

The next time an excuse starts to come out of your mouth, remember this: your customers simply don't want to hear about it. Period. They don't care what it is–they just want what they paid for.

I could write my own Excuse Book. My clients have given me thousands of reasons for why they failed financially, and most seem to think the failure was out of their control. If they had simply taken charge of their businesses instead of pointing fingers, many of these businesses would be open today.

Computer systems crash. Employees leave or get sick. Interest rates go up. Some customers are unreasonable. The economy takes a dive. Democrats get into office. Republicans get into office. Competition opens down the road. You get sick. Your family gets sick. The electricity goes off. You run out of pencils. Your dog eats your tax records.

Deal with the problems you can solve, and don't worry about what's out of your control. Accept that business life isn't always fair ... and decide to succeed anyway.

Everything Can't Stay the Same

Legendary restaurant entrepreneur Norman Brinker started as a busboy with Jack in the Box. In a survey, 88 percent of his peers rated him as the best restaurant CEO in America. That's an amazing statistic, given how many other great choices there are in that field. Brinker's philosophy: "Renew and reinvigorate your operations on a regular basis. Don't be afraid to change."

The words, "That's the way we've always done it," are a death sentence to a business today. An optimistic attitude and a willingness to learn and change are vital. If you are willing to grow personally, your business–a reflection of you–also will evolve.

Today's world economy and new technologies make it more important than ever for business owners to change to stay competitive. Local entrepreneurs can no longer afford to ignore international events.

I have a client in his mid-50s who owned an auto parts store. Tom started as a mechanic and, through hard work and perseverance, built his own company. A few years ago, his customers started disappearing faster than gas through a ruptured fuel line, and Tom didn't know why. His cash flow evaporated, he couldn't pay his rent and he drained his savings. He had to close his doors. Tom had not recognized the global competition that was affecting his business.

How can the world economy affect a local auto parts store?

One of the people who put Tom out of business turns out to be my new neighbor from Taiwan. Mr. Wong bought his house for $650,000 and immediately added a pool and boat dock–paying cash for all of it. This interested me.

He said he could not afford real estate in Taiwan because land prices had risen too high. However, his money was worth quite a bit more in the United States. In fact, he considers land in Texas to be inexpensive!

Mr. Wong, an auto parts broker, studied in Taiwan and finished his education in the States. While in the U.S., he realized how inexpensively auto parts could be made in Taiwan, and he saw a great opportunity. He now ships parts from Taiwan to the U.S. in large volumes. Only in his late 20s, Mr. Wong is making a seven-figure income annually.

Meanwhile, Tom, unaware of Mr. Wong, never guessed international competition would kill his business. He grew up in a small Texas town, which became a suburb of Dallas and Ft. Worth over time because of urban sprawl. His market changed. His competition changed. Customers now buy from Mr. Wong at one-third of the price, and get their parts more quickly.

This could not have happened without the monumental communication advances of this decade. Technology such as the Internet now makes international trade possible for small businesses. A friend of mine owns a company that sells athletic shoes. His company manufactures the shoes in Russia, where labor is cheap, and sells them in the United States. Most customers have no idea where the shoes are made.

With the relaxation of trade barriers throughout the world and advancing technologies, small-business owners must accept global influence as a reality and study its effects on their businesses.

Businesses need to keep abreast of the latest technology. Adding sales slips by hand might have worked fine 30 years ago, but when your enterprise is growing, you can't accurately manage inventory and accounts that way. Yet, many businesses continue to do this because they always have done it that way. Let technology help you do your job better.

Believe me, I understand the fear of technology. Last year, my son sat me down in front of the computer and kept me there until I learned (first, I had to learn to type). I tried to use the excuse that I had to mop the floor. But he's learned to not to take any excuses, and now I wonder how I ever survived without my computer.

Across our land, large national homebuilders are squeezing out smaller companies. Why? Because the larger companies record every tiny detail of the cost of a home on computer spreadsheets. The large companies can buy materials in greater volumes, and use cutting-edge software to control costs and make fatter profits.

Successful business owners do not resist change. For example, one homebuilder noticed new construction slowing down. After studying the market, he decided to do home remodeling until the climate changed. He succeeded and weathered the market downswing, while many homebuilders who felt remodeling was beneath their expertise did not survive. They were inflexible.

The old adage, "If it ain't broke, don't fix it," does not work anymore. Smart owners know "it" can break quickly today, and they are prepared.

Do What It Takes

You must be involved in your business, be persistent, avoid excuses and be willing to learn and change to obey The Second Commandment: Understand the Entrepreneurial Mindset.

Remember the saying, "If it doesn't kill me, it makes me stronger." Don't use the excuse that you weren't born an entrepreneur. Nobody was. It takes work, experience and all the unique talents you can muster to realize your dream. Often, as the example of Mr. Roper's mosquito house success shows, a strong desire to succeed will overcome weaknesses in other areas.

You can read books and attend seminars. You can take courses at your local college to learn how to be a good manager, use computers, organize your business or write a business plan. You can use professional accountants and attorneys to guide you. You can hire good employees to help you.

Begin with the right mindset and a fair share of knowledge, and go from there. Then, like Anna who came to this country with nothing and ended up with a successful bakery, you can say, "It's mine. I did it!"

Exercise One

Running a business requires a different mindset from working a job. Following are 20 questions you should ask yourself if you are considering starting a business.

1. Do you have organizing ability?
2. Are you in good health, and are you able to endure long hours?
3. Are you self-motivated?
4. Are you psychologically ready to take some risks?
5. Do you have faith in your abilities?
6. Do you have will power and self-discipline?
7. Are you prepared to wait months (or longer) before you make a profit?
8. Do you have specific expertise in the business you want to start, and will you commit to ongoing learning?
9. Do you know how to find your particular niche in the market, and how to identify your customers?
10. Are you open to change?
11. Do you have plenty of common sense?
12. Do you consider yourself to be a leader?

13. Do you enjoy challenges?
14. Can you deal with uncertainty?
15. Are you competitive?
16. Do you know how to sell enough of what you have, at a price that will return an adequate profit for you?
17. Can you obtain the money you will need to start and keep the business running without getting into cash-flow problems?
18. Do you like to think ahead and plan for your future, then make it happen?
19. Can you handle rejection and failure, and learn from it?
20. Do you like to make decisions?

Scoring: Although there are no guarantees, if you answered yes to the majority of these, you might have what it takes. If not, you might want to rethink your plans, perhaps take some time to think about whether the entrepreneurial life is for you.

The Third Commandment

"Once the toothpaste is out of the tube, it is awfully hard to get it back in."

—H.R. Haldeman, Watergate Senate hearings

The following is an all-too-common scene in my office:

"I really enjoy my business. It's very successful!"

"What is your salary?"

"Oh–I don't take anything out."

"How long has this been going on?"

"Three years. It's not my business that is in trouble–that's great! All my business bills are paid. It's me–my credit card charges and cash advances are enormous. I've had to pay all my living expenses with credit cards. So, I'm in trouble, but my business is fine."

This is one example of cash flow that doesn't flow. If you aren't paying yourself for the time you spend in your business, something is wrong. If you regularly use credit cards to finance your business, you are trying to climb a greased fireman's pole.

A stagnant business will die. Just as a river must flow to create life-giving oxygen to support the life within it, so must the cash in a business flow. You must understand your cash flow and plan accordingly.

Joan, 45, runs a landscaping service for a large home-building company. She rushes to my office for our meeting, and apologizes for her grass-stained overalls and worn shoes. She is an entrepreneur who loves her work and is minding the store, but there's a problem with her business plan–she doesn't have one. "Marguerite, I love my work, but the cash flow kills me," she says. "It takes me 45 days to collect on a job, and my workers need their money every Friday. I can never catch up."

Joan's options were to talk to the homebuilder to set up a faster pay schedule, see a banker about a credit line, or mix in other jobs that paid immediately.

If you are running a hot-dog stand, you'll get paid immediately when you deliver the product. This is true of many retail businesses. However, what are you going to do if the majority of your annual sales come in a three-month period? Or, what if you work in a field such as consulting, where you might spend months on a project and not get paid until after the work is completed?

The Small Business Administration reports that failure to properly plan cash flow is one of the leading causes of small-business failures. In fact, profitable businesses go bust all the time for this reason. Your business needs a sufficient cash flow to pay monthly bills, serve as a cushion in case of unexpected emergencies, provide capital for investment, and to save your credit rating.

Understand the Operating Cycle

Cash flows through a system known as an operating cycle, which includes everything from the purchase of inventory–your products–through the collection of accounts receivable–money owed to your business from sales and other sources.

Say, for example, that you own a pet supply store. Your operating cycle begins with both cash and inventory–dog food, cat toys, bird cages and so on–on hand. You don't want your shelves to run empty as you make sales, so you need to stock additional supplies in your storeroom. You buy this inventory–extra bags of Puppy Yummies, extra scratching posts, etc.–ahead of time, on credit.

As you sell those bags of Puppy Yummies, those scratching posts and other products, you will receive some revenue in cash. Other sales revenues will come to you on credit, which might be paid 30 days (or more) after the purchase date. When you finally pay for the inventory you bought on credit, you reduce both your cash and your accounts payable–the money your business owes for bills, product purchases and other expenses. Thirty days after selling those bird cages on credit, you collect your receivables, which increases your cash. Your cash has moved through the operating cycle, which then repeats itself.

Analyzing your cash flow should show whether your daily operations generate enough cash to meet your obligations. It should also show how major outflows of cash to pay your debts compare to inflows of cash from sales. The answer will tell you whether you have a positive cash flow–more flowing in than out–or a net drain. Tracking your cash flow also will help you monitor any significant changes over time. If you understand this process, you can plan for the future and prepare for business growth.

As a rule, you should have enough cash on hand each month to pay the cash obligations of the following month. By projecting your cash flow monthly, you can track and manage cash surpluses or deficiencies. You should also compare each month's actual cash flow to your previous projections. When you find deficiencies, you need to alter your business plan to come up with more cash. When you find excess cash–of course, a pleasant surprise–you might discover you've been borrowing too much, or hoarding money that could better be invested.

Let It Flow

You can increase your cash flow by using some of the following methods:

- **Collect receivables.** Actively manage your accounts receivable–money owed to you–and work quickly to collect overdue accounts. You stand to lose revenues if you do not collect aggressively. I know a doctor who actually carries $325,000 worth of receivables, most more than six months old. He said he doesn't have time to collect them. After three months, do you think a customer will send in a check voluntarily? The longer your customer's balance remains unpaid, the less likely you are to receive full payment. Upgrading your accounting software might help you stay better organized and send out your invoices on time.

- **Tighten credit requirements.** When you make your credit terms tougher, more customers must pay cash for purchases. That increases your cash on hand and reduces bad-debt expense. Be careful, though. While tightening credit terms helps in the short run, it might not benefit you in the long haul; looser credit allows more customers the opportunity to purchase your products or services. If you tighten your credit terms, watch for any drop in sales. If you ease your credit requirements, keep track of any related increase in bad-debt expenses.

- **Cut off deadbeats.** Yes, you need business, but not from people or companies who aren't paying you. Don't be fooled twice, three times–if a customer isn't paying, stop sending products or performing services until the account is squared away. If a customer has bad credit, consider putting him on cash-on-delivery for a period before you extend credit again.

- **Use early payment discounts.** You might wish to institute such a policy to get clients to pay more quickly. Use cau-

tion, however: some clients will take the discount and still send payments in beyond the early-bird window.
- **Charge late fees.** Customers going beyond the credit window? You can require them to pay a penalty when they pass the due date.
- **Take out short-term loans.** Loans from financial institutions are often necessary to cover short-term cash-flow problems. Your options can include revolving credit lines and equity loans.
- **Keep salaries down early on.** At the opposite end of the spectrum from the business owner who doesn't pay herself anything is the one who pays herself a ridiculous salary from the early days of the enterprise. Keep your salaries modest until you can truly afford to do otherwise.
- **Consider leasing high-ticket items.** Your costs might be higher, but leasing can free up cash or credit lines you would be better off using elsewhere in your business.
- **Serve clients in ways better suited to your needs.** Instead of charging project by project, can you serve some clients on retainer, which will provide you guaranteed revenues every month? Or can you set up a standing order program with your existing customers, so you will have a certain amount of guaranteed sales?
- **Spend wisely.** When you're self-elevated to CEO of your own company, you might be tempted to run out, lease the biggest office you can find, and furnish it with solid-oak desks and top-of-the-line computer systems and software. Be careful here ... especially with purchases such as furniture that will have nothing to do with your business success. Get a few quotes before you buy anything. Don't buy anything you don't really need–how satisfied will your ego be if you run yourself out of business because of foolish spending?
- **Don't overhire.** Get the most out of yourself and your staff before adding employees. Many companies hire far too many people early on and get themselves into cash-flow trouble quickly. If you have too much work, consider using independent contractors instead.

• **Increase sales.** This approach might sound like a no-brainer, but be careful. Increased sales would appear to increase your cash flow. But if you make many of your extra sales on credit, you increase your accounts receivable–money owed to you–not your cash. Meanwhile, selling more inventory means you must replace more inventory–you don't want those shelves empty, do you? If you put out more money to pay for more products, but don't collect on the extra sales for 30 days, you could deplete your firm's cash reserves. Be sure this tactic for increasing cash flow doesn't backfire on you.

• **Hold a garage sale.** Sell outdated equipment and other assets you don't need.

• **Unplug products on life support.** Some products just aren't carrying their weight anymore. Why let them drag down the rest of the company?

• **Recycle.** Boxes, bags, computer disks, paper. Whatever you can use again, use again.

• **Raise prices.** Higher prices don't always scare away customers; in fact, some companies do more business when they hike prices. Many customers expect a company to raise prices slightly every so often to keep up with inflation.

• **Control inventory.** By offering fat discounts for high-volume purchases, vendors might tempt you to take on more product than you need. The result: too much of your cash is tied up in inventory. Many business owners also purchase too much product because they're overly optimistic. Don't buy too much–it will cost you in the long run. Use better computer software or make procedural changes to make sure you are buying the right amount of product and reordering at the proper times.

Joan, the landscaper, also needed to get to work writing a sound business plan.

A business plan helps the owner focus on her goals and how to get there, and projects cash flow, including the financing a business requires.

If you're a small-business owner, one fact is certain:
1. You need a written business plan.
And a second thing is probable:
2. You don't have one.

Why Entrepreneurs Avoid Planning

A USA TODAY survey reported that only 28 percent of companies questioned had business plans, but those 28 percent had 100 percent higher profits than the other companies.

If business plans are so important, why do business owners avoid writing them ... unless they must to raise capital?

1. Goal setting is unfamiliar and, therefore, uncomfortable. Most of my business clients have never written goals and plans for their personal or business lives. When I ask why, they usually tell me they don't know how, or are afraid the plan will be wrong. There is no wrong–it's your life, and you are writing your own book, the way you want it. As for the how-tos, we'll get to that in a moment.

2. People are afraid they will get trapped in a plan. A business plan or personal plan is a guideline. It should provide for your immediate needs, as well as project future goals and serve as an inspiration so you can remember the big picture when you're trudging through the swamps. The plan must be flexible. Life is not rigid, and we've already discussed how quickly business is changing today. A good business plan leaves room for change, as well as for the unexpected.

Plans are maps, not traps.

3. People resist planning and goal-setting, because they fear the future. If the present is great, people resist planning because they think it isn't necessary: "Let's not jinx the future!" If the present looks bleak, people resist planning because they fear what could happen: "If the business is in trouble now, how can we possibly plan for the future?"

The future is inevitable. How do you want it to turn out, for yourself and for your business?

4. Entrepreneurs say they are too busy. First, they get wrapped up in the logistical details of setting up a business. Then, they say they are too busy with the day-to-day details. They don't realize that the time dedicated toward a business plan is time well spent.

Exercise: Develop Your Business Plan

There are entire books and software programs about how to write a business plan. If you feel you need help beyond this chapter, by all means, consult some of these–especially if you are going to use your plan to obtain financing. I have listed several recommended resources in the back of this book. Whatever you use as a guide, be sure to write your plan your way, and incorporate whatever you wish. It is, after all, your life and your business.

Schedule quiet time to perform the following exercise, reading the explanations, then answering the questions after each step. No TV, no phone, no kids. If you don't have all the facts now, you might need to do additional research. Be patient–writing a sound business plan takes time.

1. Describe your business. Outline your mission statement. The mission statement is vital–you should spend plenty of time developing this. It is the guiding philosophy behind your business. You should make your mission statement clear and concise. Then, take one or two paragraphs to elaborate on your mission statement.

Mission statement examples:

Chrysler Corp.: "To produce cars and trucks that people will want to buy, will enjoy driving and will want to drive again."

Autodesk Inc.: "To create quality software solutions and support services that foster innovation, creativity and productivity for customers and partners around the world."

Advest Inc.: "Advest's mission is to be the best at helping people build wealth, primarily toward retirement, through the highest quality, most effective professionals in the industry."

• **What is my mission?**

2. Describe the principals. Think about what each will contribute to the business in time, money and expertise, as well as what each will be paid.

• **Who are the owners?**
• **How many hours a week will the owners devote to the business?**
• **How many dollars will the owners invest to start the business?**
• **What knowledge and skills will the owners provide to the business?**
• **How much will the owners be paid (weekly, monthly or annually)?**

3. Outline operations. What is your business' legal structure? Explain how the business will be managed daily. Discuss hiring and personnel procedures, as well as legal requirements.

• **Will my business be a sole proprietorship, partnership or corporation?**
• **Who will handle daily business operations?**
• **What local, state and federal regulations will my business need to follow?**

4. Write a marketing plan. Describe your products and services. Also, take an in-depth look at your business name, because marketing begins with a name.

• How will I reach potential customers, present my business as unique and top the competition?
• Who is my competition, and what are my advantages and disadvantages?
• What is the market for my product or service, including size, location and demographics?
• What is my advertising budget?
• Does my business name convey to the public what I do?
• Does my name convey the image I want?
• Is the name easy to spell and remember?
•What is my product pricing strategy?

5. Describe location, inventory and equipment needs.

• What is the best location for my business?
• What is the most efficient layout of the offices?
• What inventory and equipment must I purchase to start the business?
• What will I buy in coming months and years?
• What are my expansion plans?

6. Outline staffing needs and training plans.

• How many employees will I need?
• Will they be temporary, part-time or full-time employees, or independent contractors?
• What are their job descriptions?
• What will they be paid?
• How much on-the-job training will I provide?
• How will my business further continuing education?
• What will employee policies be?
• When will I add new employees?

7. Explain the sources and amount of startup capital.

• **Where's the money coming from?**
• **Would colleagues or friends lend me money?**
• **Who could I approach to invest as silent partners?**
• **Is there anyone I can approach who would want to become a stockholder in my company?**
• **What venture capitalists might lend my company money?**

8. Estimate start-up costs.

• **What upfront investments do I need to make (for example, franchise fees)?**
• **What equipment will I need to buy?**
• **What other supplies will I need?**
• **How much will I spend to get the word out about my new business?**

9. Project operating expenses.

• **What is overhead (rent, leasing costs, loan payments)?**
• **What will my labor costs be?**

10. Outline your cash flow. This shows what money is coming into your business and what expenses you must pay. At the end of each month, you will show either a profit or loss, and that is carried over to the next month's cash-flow projections. If you are showing losses, you probably need additional money.

• **What are my cash flow projections ...**
... each month in the first year?
... each quarter in the second year?
... annually in the third year and beyond?
• **What are my future financing needs, and how will I satisfy them?**

11. Provide an income statement. An income statement, based on elements such as revenue, expenses and cost of goods, shows how much your company makes or loses during the year. Subtract both cost of goods and expenses from revenue to arrive at a net profit or loss.

- **What are my income projections ...**
  ... each month in the first year?
  ... each quarter in the second year?
  ... annually in the third year and beyond?
- **What will my net profit or loss be ...**
  ... in the first year?
  ... in the second year?
  ... in the third year and beyond?

12. Develop a balance sheet. Do one for each year of business. This summarizes all the previous information and breaks it into assets–what you own–and liabilities–what you owe. Calculate your equity by subtracting total liabilities from total assets. This balance sheet is an important tool for potential investors when you are seeking financing.

13. What is your break-even point? That is, at what point will you be earning at least as much as you've put into your business and, hopefully, start making a profit?

14. List other goals for the coming month, six months, year, and three years.

15. Brainstorm potential obstacles and possible solutions.

After you write your business plan, review it once a day for 10 days to see if there's anything you missed. Then, run it by your attorney and accountant, and perhaps a business consultant, to get their input.

Once you're running your business, review your plan frequently to see how it compares to projections. You will need to adjust your plan often as unexpected situations arise, or as you see new opportunities you had not considered when you first wrote the plan. Often, when you start down a pathway toward realizing your goals, a new, more exciting and profitable path will appear. Do not hesitate to turn in another direction if it is right for you and your business.

The Fourth Commandment

Comply With Tax Laws: Render Unto Caesar!

"Render therefore unto Caesar the things which are Caesar's and unto God, the things that are God's."
— St. Matthew, *Holy Bible*

"A Government which robs Peter to pay Paul can always depend on the rapport of Paul."
— George Bernard Shaw, *Everybody's Political What's What*

Story One

"John, come look! Oh, my gosh! What in the world! John, hurry! Come now!" John rolled his eyes, and slowly put down his stained coffee cup and tuna sandwich. After 30 years of living and working with his wife, he'd learned not to react so quickly to her insistent commands. Mary stared out of the window of their auto repair shop, which had just closed for the evening.

"John, they have black hoods on their heads–and guns! A whole van load of 'em!"

"What are you talking about, Mary?"

John was on the move now. The slam of his desk chair hitting the thinly carpeted concrete floor couldn't be heard over the commotion outside.

Persistent knocking began at the front door.

"Mary, quick, go to the back of the shop–call the police!" The knocking continued. Someone finally shouted, "Police! Open up. Federal IRS agents. We have a seizure to carry out."

John opened the door. Ten men with black hoods on their heads walked in and proceeded to load all his shop equipment, furniture and inventory into waiting trucks. They even took the picture of the Grand Canyon off the wall. It was a photograph of Mary and John smiling, looking up from the bottom amid the brilliant red rocks. It was shot by an obliging tourist 35 years ago, while the couple were on their honeymoon.

Story Two

"Mr. Gonzalez, here's the $25,000 check you requested. Now, if you'll go ahead and take the padlock off the building, I'd appreciate it. I have some big clients coming in today to go over the plans for a mall they are building. It's cold out here in the wind, and this is all quite embarrassing. I appreciate you working with us on the $10,000 balance left on my firm's taxes. We are world-renowned architects, you know, and we just need a little time."

Gonzalez, a lead IRS agent, takes the check, unlocks the door and gestures back toward the parking lot: "Is that your Porsche?"

"Yes, it's my pride and joy," the architect says with a smile.

"Give me the keys," Gonzalez demands.

"Oh, it belongs to me, not to our business," the architect responds nervously. "Our business is a corporation, you know."

"Don't care," Gonzalez says. "I said give me the keys. I'm going to take it as security for payment of the remaining taxes your corporation owes the IRS."

The architect hands Gonzalez the keys. Seconds later, Gonzalez is gone, happily racing out of the parking lot in the architect's pride and joy.

Story Three

Tom's business fell deep into tax debt, and he took a licking at an audit. He set up a payment plan, and fought and scraped each month to make the payments on time. One afternoon, an IRS agent wanders into his store, announces it is closed and demands that Tom triple his monthly payments to the government.

"Look, we had a deal," Tom protests. "We are making the agreed payments and are always on time. How in the world do you expect me to triple my tax payments after you shut my business down?"

The agent shrugs, leads Tom outside, slaps a padlock on the front door and leaves.

Story Four

"George, can you drive faster? I'm in pain! This doesn't feel right. The third baby is supposed to be easy, but it feels like something is wrong!"

"Hold on, Nancy. Almost there ... here we are, sweetheart. I'll pull right up to the Emergency Room door. Everything's going to be fine."

"George ... what's that yellow tape on the door?"

"Looks like a police barricade or something," George says.

George runs to the Emergency Room door. No one's around. A handwritten sign on the door says, "Hospital Closed–IRS Levy."

"They can't shut down a hospital," George mutters to himself, "Can they?"

How many of these four stories are true?

Not only are all four true, they all happened to my clients!

What's wrong in all of these pictures? Somebody did not pay taxes.

Pay Your Taxes

The Internal Revenue Service has more power than any other federal agency–and that's when the IRS is playing by the rules. And, as we have seen by Congressional hearings, the agency often has not played by the rules. State tax agencies can be equally powerful and aggressive.

I have seen more small businesses fail because taxes aren't properly accounted for and paid than for any other reason.

The following scene occurs in my office at least once a week. At least once a week!

Client: "I'm not worried about the IRS closing me down. I'm paying on the back taxes under an installment agreement. If the IRS closed me down and auctions everything, it won't pay off my taxes, so they will surely leave my business open so I can pay them. That only makes sense, doesn't it?"

Client (weeks or months later): "Marguerite–I can't believe they would do that! The IRS locked up my business. HELP!"

By this point, if you are this client, you are in deep trouble. If I can give you only three words of business advice, they would be these: PAY YOUR TAXES.

Take advantage of all legitimate tax deductions, but pay the IRS and other taxing agencies every cent you owe. If you think you can duck taxes until you get caught, then negotiate with the IRS–forget it. If you think you shouldn't have to pay taxes because they are "unconstitutional," that's all well and good, but your business will be closed by the IRS, and you just might find yourself in prison, to boot. If you think the nice people at the IRS will be understanding when you tell them you're just running a little ol' business and you don't know about complicated things like tax laws, think again.

Caesar doesn't care. Caesar just wants his share. And he will get it.

If you think I'm telling you these stories to scare you ... you are right. Operating a business and ignoring or neglecting taxes is a direct route to business failure. You must find out about what taxes you owe, and hire professionals to ensure the appropriate taxes are being paid. On time. Every time.

Our hearts go out to John and Mary for having the government walk in and put an end to a life's work. But the bottom line is this: it was no one's fault but their own. They didn't pay enough taxes, the IRS sent them plenty of warnings and notices, and they ignored it all, guessing the IRS would go away. This policy gets you a van full of hooded agents with guns.

Your CPA will help you with your books and prepare your tax returns, but you can't leave everything to her. It's your responsibility to understand all taxes that must be paid, and have a system in place to ensure correct accounting and timely payments. Blaming your CPA isn't going to get you off the hook with taxing agencies if there are problems. And, believe me, dealing with taxing agencies is ... well ... taxing.

Before you start a business–or now, if you have a business and are unsure–call your city, county, state and federal governments to see what taxes apply to you. Many government agencies hold free seminars about taxes for small-business owners, and a good number have websites with helpful information.

Let's take a look at taxes common to most businesses, beginning with those at the federal level. Taxes vary, depending on where you live and what you do, so do your homework. Your type of business organization–sole proprietorship, partnership, C-Corporation or S-Corporation–also will affect your taxes, and I'll touch on that briefly here. If you're not sure what your business structure is, or should be, see The Eighth Commandment for details.

Federal Taxes
Federal Identification

You need a taxpayer identification number so the IRS can process your returns. The most common kinds of identification are your Social Security number and an employer identification number (EIN).

If you have any employees, operate your business as a corporation or partnership, have a Keogh plan, or file employment, excise, alcohol, tobacco or firearms tax returns, you need an EIN. You can obtain the application form (SS-4) from IRS or Social Security Administration offices. Make sure you apply for your EIN well before you have to file a return or make a tax deposit. If you don't receive your number in time, file your returns anyway and write in the EIN space that the number is applied for.

Federal Withholding

Be sure to obtain a Social Security number from each of your employees, and record the information exactly as it appears on their Social Security cards. If the employee's name is not correct–which often happens because of marriages and divorces–ask the employee to request a new card from the Social Security Administration. If you make payments to independent contractors, make sure to obtain their Social Security numbers for informational filings.

Each time you pay employee wages, you are required to withhold a certain percentage of money based on the number of exemptions an employee claims and his wage level. The IRS will furnish charts that show what you must withhold. This money must be paid to the IRS according to a timetable. Use the employee's Form W-4 and use the methods discussed in IRS Publication 15.

Whenever small businesses get into financial crunches, they often turn to this pool of money withheld but not yet turned over to the government. The thinking goes like this: "Let's see ... I have a tax deposit due at the bank on the 15th. This is just the fifth, and I have to pay these bills. By the 15th, at least three of my accounts will have paid me, so I'll have my tax deposit."

Don't touch it! This is treated as a trust fund by the IRS, and the agency is not pleased when money you took from employees to pay the government doesn't show up on time. Don't mess with withholding monies.

FICA and Medicare

In addition to withholding income tax, you must also withhold the amount required for the Federal Insurance Contribution Act, commonly known as Social Security. Social Security coverage provides you with future retirement benefits, disability benefits, survivor benefits and medical insurance (Medicare). You, as an employer, must match the amount of FICA you withhold from employees' paychecks, and all of this must be sent to the IRS. You also must withhold money and match the amount for Medicare. This is discussed in IRS Publication 15.

If you are self-employed, you will pay your share of these taxes through self-employment tax. The IRS levies stiff penalties if these payments and the required returns are not on time.

Federal Unemployment Tax

This tax is part of the federal and state program under the Federal Unemployment Tax Act that pays unemployment compensation to workers who lose their jobs. You pay this only from your own funds; employees are not responsible for this tax.

Federal Income Tax

All businesses except partnerships must file an annual income tax return (partnerships file an information return). Which form you use depends on how your business is organized.

The federal income tax is pay-as-you go—you have to pay taxes as you earn or receive income throughout the year. Employees usually have income tax withheld from their pay. If you don't have income tax withheld, or if you aren't paying enough tax this way, you might have to pay estimated taxes.

Usually, sole proprietors, partners, and shareholders of S-Corporations pay taxes on income by making regular payments of estimated taxes throughout the year. These payments are usually quarterly. If you don't have to make estimated payments, you may pay any taxes due when you file your annual return. See IRS Publication 505 for details.

Corporate Income Tax

If your business is incorporated, and treated as a C-Corporation, you will draw a regular salary and be subject to withholding the same as your other employees. If you elect to be treated as an S-Corporation for tax purposes, you will not be paid a salary, but all the profits and losses of the corporation will flow through to you. So, you will need to make estimated payments. You should give your business structure a great deal of thought, and be sure to include your tax attorneys and CPA in the discussions.

State Taxes

Income Tax

Some, but not all, states have income taxes similar to the federal government's.

Other states tax corporate income only. This may be called a franchise tax if the state constitution prohibits income tax.

Sales Tax

If your business is in retail sales, you will be taxed by the state on your gross sales. Sales of certain items might be exempt from tax. Certain services also might be taxed. This area can be a minefield for a small business–make sure you have clear answers about when you must collect sales tax. Then be sure you have good computer software for keeping detailed records of your sales ... in case you are audited. The laws vary depending on which state you are doing business in.

Alcohol Tax

If you serve alcohol to patrons or sell it retail, you will be required to pay alcohol tax. This differs from sales tax and is reported to a different agency.

Other Taxes

Property Tax

The city, county, school district, water district, fire district and other local taxing districts in which you do business may assess taxes on your business and personal holdings. These taxes can be substantial.

These are the common taxes, but your business might be subject to other taxes and fees.

Remember to work tax payments into your business plan. You often have to pay taxes long before you receive payment for goods, and this can wreak havoc on your cash flow.

If your existing business is behind in tax payments, the Financial First Aid Kit at the back of this book will explain some common terms, as well as your options. If necessary, meet with a tax attorney or business reorganization specialist. Don't put it off–take care of the matter now, before you have a story similar to the four at the beginning of this chapter.

Know what taxes you must pay.

Pay your taxes.

Exercise

If you are starting a business, make sure you contact all federal, state and local agencies to determine which taxes you have to pay. Don't assume anything–one overlooked tax could run you out of business down the road. If you're already in business, check to make sure you are paying all of your taxes, and that you're doing so promptly. Also, commit to this statement: "I will never dip into the withholding pool to cover cash flow problems."

The Fifth Commandment

Expect the Unexpected: Learn to Recognize Problems, and Take Action to Solve Them

"Everything has got a moral, if you can only find it."
—Lewis Carroll, *Alice's Adventures in Wonderland*

It wasn't long ago that Alice couldn't wait for Steve the postman to walk through the doors of her gift shop every day. Now, it's a dreaded event. Alice watched with apprehension as Steve tossed the day's mail on her desk. The shop, which she owned with her husband, Charles, was not doing well financially lately. Alice scanned the mail to see if any of her charge account customers had sent checks. No such luck. Another stack of bills.

Charles started this business 12 years ago. They had succeeded in putting their two children through college, and had considered their enterprise a success. But today, the shop rent was officially two months behind, and Alice couldn't pay it.

In his ignorance, Charles believed all was well, but Alice hadn't paid their business suppliers in two months. She hadn't paid their house payment in three months. Their personal car and business truck payments were two months behind. She had used all of their credit-card advances to support the business. No more credit was available.

Feeling sick, hopeless and out of control, Alice wondered what had happened to the dreams they had when they first married. How did they get into this trouble, and what could help? If the business did so well for more than a decade, and they were doing everything the same, what had happened?

Prepare for Ups ... and Downs

A Mack truck is headed straight at Alice and Charles, and they're staring right at it and refusing to budge. If you are in financial trouble, don't just stand there–do something!

Every business has its cycles, its ups and downs. Prepare for them, then the unexpected won't shock you.

Have you ever learned a risky sport, such as scuba diving, sky diving, rock climbing or, the riskiest of all, driving on America's roads? You constantly practice what to do when you get in trouble. You are taught safety and emergency measures, as well as to know your limits.

To expect the unexpected, you first must be able to see the warning signs of a troubled business. Second, realize our culture encourages beliefs in dreams, but some of the same personality traits that help you succeed as an entrepreneur might do your business in because they prevent you from recognizing trouble. Third, acknowledge our culture sees bankruptcy as a moral issue, but it can be a way out of trouble if nothing else will work.

Clothes-ing Time

Bob operates a men's retail clothing store that had been successful for five years. In the last two years, the city's economy grew depressed, and his store suffered. To increase business, Bob expanded his advertising and reduced prices. He sold his most desirable items but, after paying bills, he did not have enough cash to purchase new merchandise. He was unable to pay advertising bills, so his creditors cut him off. His cash flow ceased. He used the money set aside for employees' taxes to pay wages. The IRS caught on, audited him, and levied on his business.

Prescription for Trouble

Angelo, a doctor, had a booming medical practice. However, he failed to keep proper accounting records and pay his quarterly taxes on time. When he filed his tax returns late, the bill was so staggering he could not pay it. The IRS threatened to seize his office equipment and homestead. Angelo had to file a business reorganization in bankruptcy court so he could continue in practice and have enough time to pay the IRS. Years later, he is struggling to repay this debt.

Alice and Charles, and Bob and Angelo, waited so long to recognize problems that they had to seek bankruptcy court protection. All would have solved their situations in simpler ways if they knew the warning signs of business trouble.

Evidence of financial problems appears in different ways. As Alice did, some people shuffle bills each month because they can't make a full payment. They keep the business going by paying bills in Group A one month and those in Group B the next. They borrow to the hilt on their credit-card cash advance lines, only to eventually run out of credit. They might send $5 or $10 payments to creditors to show they are attempting to pay, hoping this will stop harassing phone calls. Unfortunately, this does not work.

They pay business creditors but ignore the house payment because the mortgage company does not call until the owner is about three payments behind. They ignore payroll taxes because the IRS usually doesn't come knocking until you are about a year behind. The tax bill is large, and owners are sure the financial stress is temporary. After all, the big contract is always around the corner.

If any of this sounds familiar, you are showing signs of financial problems and might benefit by seeking help now. Sit down with your accountant and take a realistic look at the financial status of your business and personal life. Make sure all financial records are up to date. Then, make an appointment with an attorney who specializes in business reorganization and explore your financial options.

Early action gets better results. Seek advice soon.

Warning Signs

Some of the first warning signs of trouble are often subtle and are missed by management. Look for these signals:

• **Unhappy employees.** Are your employees dissatisfied or not performing well as a whole? Disgruntled employees are a sure sign of troubles to come.

• **Salespeople problems.** Are your salespeople making enough money to keep them motivated? Do you have too many salespeople for the workload?

• **Slow-paying customers.** Are the majority of your customers paying you regularly? Often, if a customer is dissatisfied with service or a product, he won't say so but will avoid the bill. If many of your customers are delinquent, your company might be slipping.

• **Reduction in sales volume** that cannot be attributed to normal business cycles.

• **Inability to pay debts** as they are due, including owners' salaries.

• **A depressed industry** as a whole.

• **Not enough cash flow** to keep the business open much longer.

• **Demands by suppliers** or creditors for cash on delivery, lawsuits filed by creditors, or demands for additional security by creditors.

• **Competition** that has caused important customers to go elsewhere.

Every entrepreneur hates to face the reality of financial problems. But facing the problem is a major step toward solving it. Avoid the ostrich syndrome of sticking your head in the sand. If you are in trouble, don't just stand there–do something! You can conquer major financial problems if you know what to do. Expect the unexpected, and know your options.

Warning Signs of Financial Trouble and Where to Go for Help

You can't recognize trouble unless you know what to look for. I've devised three classifications that can help you decide how serious your financial problems are–the Green, Yellow and Red zones.

Green Zone

In the Green Zone, you might not even feel as if you have financial problems. But it's important to recognize problem areas, seek expert advice and plan accordingly. The Green Zone includes short-term financial problems that can snowball into major long-term money woes if you don't take action now.

You might be in the Green Zone if you are experiencing any of the following:

• **Cash flow problems.** Your business is slow or the economy is stagnant. You might have enough cash to make it through the next two months, but not enough to replenish inventory.

• **A shortage of contract jobs.** You do contract work, but you do not have another job for two months, and your cash won't support you until then.

• **Unexpected taxes.** Your tax bill is larger than usual and you do not have enough to pay it and your other bills.

• **Minimum payments on bills.** You can make only the smallest allowable payments on your business accounts and cannot significantly reduce the balance.

• **Creditors demanding additional collateral.** Your bank or other creditor has agreed to consolidate and renew your past-due loans, but demands you pledge additional security.

Here is an example of a company in the Green Zone that sought help:

A nursing-home owner came to see me because the $3 million business note secured by his business was due in two weeks, and the bank had not yet agreed to renew it. All business property was pledged on this note, and the owner also had personally guaranteed the corporate debt. I called and tried to negotiate with the bank to extend the loan. I let them know that, if necessary, the company was prepared to file a Chapter 11 bankruptcy reorganization to keep the business open. The bank agreed to extend the note to keep the nursing home out of Chapter 11.

The owner sought help in time to solve the problem. Instead of just assuming the bank would renew the note, he sought help to head off a major disaster.

The threat of bankruptcy is not always necessary. In this case, I used the approach because the health of the home's residents was at stake, and the owner had to be sure he could keep operating.

The Green Zone is the best time to seek help. Recognize potential problems, and seek expert advice if necessary. You can consider consulting with an attorney, a financial adviser, CPA, consultant, creditor workout specialist or any appropriate mix of the above.

If you are feeling sick, emotionally stressed or depressed because of your business troubles, also consult with your minister, psychologist or family physician. Financial problems often cause stress, depression and an inability to sleep. You must protect your mental and physical health as fiercely as you protect your business.

After you educate yourself, you will not feel as powerless.

Most people are embarrassed to seek help because it hurts their pride. They also are afraid that their customers and suppliers will learn they can't pay their bills. In most cases, people close to you–be it family, friends or business associates–already sense you are in trouble.

If you need help, ask. Your business and health are at stake.

Yellow Zone

Truck stop

Charles, a middle-aged man wearing jeans and cowboy boots, sauntered into my office. He sat down and said, "Ms. Kirk, I have some questions about my eight-year-old trucking business. First of all, before we get started, I want you to know that I'm not interested in bankruptcy. There is no way that I will file bankruptcy, and that is not why I am here." He then went on to say, "I'm really in good shape with my creditors. I've paid everybody except for three. These three are unreasonable, so I ignore them. Why won't they give me time? Why are pressuring me? What can I do to get them off my back?"

The statement by Charles is not unusual. He has a business in trouble and doesn't want to admit it. Charles likes to believe he is satisfying all of his creditors, when in reality, he does not have enough money to go around.

Charles is in the Yellow Zone. Any of the following situations might indicate that your business is in this stage:

• **Immediate payment demands.** Your creditors require immediate payment on new deliveries, or require joint checks on jobs.

• **Creditors rejecting payment plans.** You have proposed a workout (payment plan) schedule to your creditors, but not all of them have agreed to it.

• **Heavy dependence on credit-card cash advances.** Your personal credit cards are keeping your business open. If a business can't make it on its own, you are compounding the problem with high-interest financing on personal credit cards.

• **Missed payments.** You have missed two or more payments on your lease, on business assets, on any secured property, or with a creditor.

• **Lawsuits.** You have been sued and do not have the money to finance the defense. You know the suit is legitimate, and you probably will lose.

• **Unpaid taxes.** You did not pay all your taxes when they were due, or you have not filed your returns in several years. Unless this is immediately remedied, the tax collector will close your business for you. You can bet on it!

• **Harassing creditors.** Creditors are calling constantly. This can destroy both your and your employees' morale.

• **Insufficient inventory.** You cannot stock enough inventory to keep customers interested in your merchandise.

• **Uninsured medical expenses.** You have incurred large medical bills that were not covered by your personal insurance policy. Or your employees have work-related medical bills that were not covered by private insurance or workman's compensation. If you are responsible for these bills, you must pay or face lawsuits.

• **Loan default.**

In the Yellow Zone, it is vital that you consult an attorney, CPA, and possibly a creditor workout specialist immediately. If your attorney says bankruptcy is the only option, you should seek a second opinion. Attorneys differ in how they approach problems, and some are more creative than others.

If you don't seek help when you are in the Yellow Zone, chances are good it's only a matter of time before you slide into ...

The Red Zone

If you find yourself in one of the situations listed below, you should immediately seek a business reorganization attorney for guidance. You are past the point of negotiating with your creditors. Only court protection will save you if you are experiencing one of the following:

- **IRS levy.** The IRS is threatening to levy on your property or lock up your business, or it has already levied against your property.
- **Foreclosure.** Your mortgage company is refusing to accept your payments and has indicated your property is posted for foreclosure. Or, your landlord is threatening to lock up your business for unpaid rent.
- **Repossession.** A secured creditor has told you he is planning to repossess the property held as security on his note. This could happen quickly, leaving you with no way out.
- **Judgment.** A creditor has obtained a substantial judgment against you and is seeking to sell your business or personal assets to pay it.
- **Loan called by government agency.** Your bank has been taken over by the FDIC or another government liquidating agency, and they will not renew your note. You cannot obtain other financing, and the note is secured by your valuable and necessary business assets.

In most Red Zone cases, state or federal court protection is necessary to protect you from creditors. If you do not act, you will probably lose assets and be forced into a liquidating bankruptcy. In other words, you WILL lose your business. If you act now, court protection might allow you to reorganize your business and retain control.

Why Entrepreneurs Ignore Signs of Trouble

It is a natural emotional reaction to deny the existence of a financial problem, even as the crisis develops. We tend to hope the problem will solve itself and go away. But attacking problems and seeking help early often can solve troubles before they snowball.

Business owners tend to hide their heads in the sand and refuse to see obvious money problems for several reasons:

Cultural Traits

In America, success is king. Money is a huge motivator. It can bring us security, friends, recognition by our peers and freedom to do as we wish. American culture values what can be seen, what can be flaunted, and the outside package of a person instead of his soul.

Strength of character seems unimportant.

One billboard I've seen sends this message clearly: "Make yourself happy: buy a new car from us." Why would you buy a new car if yours still ran well? Would it make you happy? Would you be as happy when the payments started?

Entrepreneurs identify themselves with their businesses. It's "J. Brown Inc." An owner's name is on the door. If the business fails, the owner might feel like a personal failure: "What will my friends think? Will I still have friends if I'm broke? What will the neighbors say? Will my children be embarrassed? Can they go to school and face their friends?" It's hard for an owner to separate his self-esteem from his business struggles. The business is a projection of the owner.

When times are tough, many owners choose to deny reality rather than admit to problems and take action. As a result, they make the reality worse and worse ... until they can no longer ignore it.

Personality Traits

The same personality traits that help an entrepreneur become successful can prevent her from acknowledging her business is in trouble until it's too late.

Entrepreneurs are optimistic risk takers. They have to believe in success. Yet this belief often hinders their ability to see problems. Because they are comfortable taking risks–or they grow moreso as they gain confidence–they often climb too far out on the financial limb to get back safely.

Entrepreneurs often treat the symptom, rather than the problem that needs solving. It's like taking aspirin for a headache. If the headache goes away, you're happy. But you haven't found the cause of the headache, which could be too much caffeine, poor diet, stress, anxiety, or a medical condition.

In the 1970s, I worked for the Environmental Protection Agency in Atlanta. After two months on the job, I started going to the local YMCA to swim at lunchtime every day. I swam for an hour and, by the time I changed, ate and returned to work, it became a two-hour lunch break. I told myself that I needed the exercise, and that heavy cigarette smoke in our office was giving me headaches.

As I later realized, these were only symptoms of my greater problem: I hated my job. I was avoiding the problem by believing what was false.

My Erroneous Beliefs

I needed the job security.
I liked my job and it had
   prestige.
I liked my co-workers.

I could use this job to do
   my part for the Earth

Truth

Other jobs were available.
I found my job boring no
   matter what title I had.
Most of the people had little
   in common with me.
I was restricted in what I
   could do because of the
   politics of the time, and I
   was frustrated by the
   system.

By holding onto my erroneous beliefs, I put myself in a bad position. After four months, I was called into my supervisor's office and told that my working style was not compatible with the agency's office atmosphere. I was fired.

It was so clear–but I didn't see it coming. After I left, I was relieved. I moved on to a job I liked, and later started my own business. In looking at this experience, I saw how I had tricked myself into accepting my behavior so I would not have to make changes. It was easier to deny my dislike of the job and avoid the issue. However, had I confronted my problem and quit, it would have been healthier for me and better for my self-esteem. I would have taken control of my life instead of handing the steering wheel over to someone else.

Entrepreneurs are Independent

Small-business owners like to think they can do everything themselves. They avoid professional advisers, thinking this will save money. Maybe they will hire an on-site bookkeeper for a low salary to avoid working with a competent accountant. But the old saying, "You get what you pay for," is so true in business.

Entrepreneurs also like to avoid lawyers. Often, a businessman will come in and tell me that his business is in great shape. He has only one problem: his main supplier has put him on a cash-only basis and, by the way, he forgot to mention the IRS is closing him down if he doesn't come up with $50,000 by noon tomorrow. His independence prevented him from seeking help earlier.

I'll talk more about this problem later. The Financial First Aid Kit at the end of the book goes into much greater detail about financial problems and options.

Remember The Fifth Commandment: Expect the Unexpected—Learn to Recognize Problems, and Take Action to Solve Them:
• Know the warning signs of a troubled business.
• Know your options.
• Know where to go for help if you need it.
• Act immediately: the longer you wait, the fewer options you have.
• Do the following exercises:

Exercise One

Review the warning signs again. If you are experiencing financial problems, turn immediately to the Financial First Aid Kit at the back for further instructions. Don't delay!

Exercise Two

How prepared are you for the unexpected? Following are some events that could potentially hurt a business. Brainstorm a little and think about what you might do to manage in these circumstances:

Natural Disasters

- Tornado
- Flood
- Hurricane
- Earthquake

- Snowstorm
- Drought
- Cold snap
- Heat wave

Financial Factors

- Rising inflation
- Unexpected increases in fees and taxes

- Skyrocketing interest rates

Technical Problems

- Computer failure
- Internet access problems

- E-mail overload
- Vehicle breakdown

Market Troubles

- Labor strike
- International embargo
- New competition
- Product price reductions

- Transportation strike
- Supply shortage
- Decreasing demand

Other

- Personal problems
- New, demanding government regulations

- Loss of office space/need to move

The Sixth Commandment

Seize Prosperity: Learn How to Create Money

"He said to His disciples, 'Therefore, I tell you do not worry about your life, what you will eat, or about your body, what you will wear. For life is more than food, and the body more than clothing ... Consider the lilies, how they grow. They neither toil nor spin, yet I tell you, even Solomon in all his glory was not clothed like one of these.' "

—St. Luke, *Holy Bible*

"If you think you can or you think you can't, either way, you are right."

—Henry Ford

My parents had a major impact on my views about money and prosperity. I was fortunate to have grown up in a family that was able to provide for all of my food and shelter needs. As a result, however, I took this for granted.

I did not equate money with prosperity. Prosperity, to me, was freedom, being able to find out who I was and what I could contribute to the world. Prosperity was having close, supportive friends, and love. My parents gave me the material things I needed, but I did not feel prosperous because, in their belief system, money was scarce and had to be controlled. In actuality, money in my family was plentiful.

To get tuition money when I went to college, I had to go to Dad's office to let him know what I needed. Mom also went to his office for her financial needs, because he would never bring the checkbook home. Dad always looked at the college bill and gave me less to see if I could make it. College costs were fixed, and there was no way for me to change them. So, I told the college officials I was allergic to most foods and could not eat in the cafeteria. That let me use my meal money to pay other bills.

My first year in college, I lived on carrots, apples and an occasional hamburger. I lost 25 pounds and felt sick and frustrated. This experience reinforced my belief that if someone supplies you with money, that gives him control over you. I grew to believe money was evil.

In truth, money is neither good nor bad. It exists just as a medium of exchange. In retrospect, both my and my father's beliefs about money were out of line. When I married and had children, I realized the comforts money could bring and started to change my views. But before I could allow true prosperity in my life, I had to go back and see why I did not believe I either needed or deserved it. This took plenty of self-examination but made all the difference. I dumped my limiting beliefs and chose to be prosperous, which has been a great asset in my business life.

As important as it is to develop a sound business plan, rooted in facts and figures that all add up, it is equally vital to believe your business will be successful. You must believe that with all your heart and soul. You must understand what prosperity means to you, believe you can achieve it, then expect and seize it.

Most people equate prosperity with money. Prosperity is really everything important to us, such as time, love, creativity, adventure and challenge. In our society, money gives us the opportunity to enjoy these.

Business owners need money. And they must learn how to create money.

I'm not talking about the kind of money creation cited as the reason why the government redesigned the $20 bill, the kind that will get you five to 10 in the federal pen. I'm referring to an active process you must go through to bring money into your life. Before we earn money, we must create it in our minds.

Entrepreneurs need to examine their beliefs about money and eliminate those that prevent them from developing wealth and prosperity.

Am I saying that entrepreneurs self-sabotage themselves and cause their businesses to fail? Absolutely. I see it all the time with my clients. Most of them have no idea that their negative beliefs about money have led directly to their business failures.

To create money, you must dump old limiting beliefs, including, "To make so much money, I need to put in so much time," "There are a limited number of customers available, so competition must hurt my business," and, "There is only so much money in the world, and every time someone makes a dollar, it's a dollar less for me."

These are all limiting beliefs that see scarcity in a world of abundance. Once you can step beyond these beliefs, you can learn to create the money you need in your life and bring prosperity.

If you see money as forever slipping from your grasp, then it will do so. If you think earning money is difficult, then it will be. Your thoughts about money define your experience with it. If you see scarcity, you will have it. If you see abundance, you will have it.

Changing Times, Changing Beliefs

We call money "currency." As with energy or electricity, money is made to flow, not to be hoarded. It is accepted as value for work performed or goods sold. Early societies had no money and simply traded for what they wanted. If you wanted an ox, you traded grain for spices, spices for cloth, then the cloth for the ox. This was all time-consuming, and difficult to fit in your back pocket.

Money began as a convenience. I grew up in Augusta, Ga., in the 1940s and 1950s, a couple thousand years after the creation of money. Our local candy store was my favorite place. With 10 pennies in my pocket, I would fling open the store's creaking screen door to view a most beautiful sight: huge barrels and jars of multicolored bubble gum, Mary Janes, Tootsie Rolls, Hershey bars, suckers and Chiclets. Candy was two pieces for one penny. Money had value I could see and taste: I went home with a hefty bag of candy.

Beliefs about money and prosperity have evolved throughout history, but have changed radically in the last 50 years. Prior to World War II in America, nine million men were unemployed and the average American left school in the eighth grade. Only 17 percent of married women worked outside the home. Credit cards were unknown. The train was the main means of travel, and air travel was inaccessible to most. Prewar suburbia was inhabited only by the wealthy, college-educated country club set, and everyone else lived in cities or on farms.

World War II, a huge economic boost to America, changed our beliefs forever. Women were necessary and accepted in the workplace. Technology gave us new materials and inventions, resulting–after the war–in greater leisure time and improved living conditions. Communications technology exploded. The idea of prosperity changed. In postwar America, everyone wanted a TV, car, refrigerator, dishwasher, washing machine and so on. With more women working, we soon began the era of the two-provider family.

The generation of adults who came through the Depression and two world wars believed in discipline, strong family bonds, church, education and a home in a nice neighborhood to raise their children, then retire and enjoy their grandchildren, and die with savings in the bank. Prosperity was accomplished by working harder and longer.

As was the case with me, ensuing generations are struggling with their relationships to money. Many of today's adults know there's something more to life beyond trading hours for dollars, such as time with family and the right to enjoy one's own life. But many repeat the same flawed work patterns their parents and grandparents followed, patterns that were successful in earning the dollar but brought little other satisfaction.

To complicate matters further, money itself is changing today. The world is starting to see paper money and coins being phased out. Increasingly, money is represented by your ATM card, your credit card and as numbers in your bank account. As if money already weren't impersonal enough.

Some stores don't even want cash anymore–it's too much trouble. I used a $100 bill to pay for a dress. The department store clerk was required to take the cash up to the office to verify it was authentic before she completed the purchase. It kept me and other customers in line waiting. Of course, I'll use my credit card next time.

You can do business worldwide today and never touch a dollar. The growing impersonality of money is making its value elusive, and further contributing to the troubles people have with the dollar.

How to Create Money

If you are doing the work you love, as The First Commandment requires, creating money becomes easier. You are already on the right path to fulfilling your destiny. But if you are doing something you hate, you will always have trouble creating money.

To help create money in your business and life, you can adopt the following nine beliefs. Begin taking an active role in creating money today:

1. I believe the money supply is infinite.

Here's a fact about money: you are never going to have it all.

Not if you're Bill Gates. Not if you're Donald Trump. Not if you run the new Internet hot-shot company.

So stop worrying about what other companies are doing and how much they have. This is your life, your business, your race. Quit keeping up with the Joneses–it's a battle you can't win. There will always be someone with a bigger business, more cash, a nicer car.

The good news is, there's enough money out there for you.

Most people view the monetary world as finite–a dime more for you means a dime less for me. It's a constant dorm-room battle for the last slice of pizza. This view contributes a great deal of stress to our lives and adds to the increasing problem we have getting along with others. It puts others in the role of your financial enemy.

In *Creating Money*, authors Sanaya Roman and Duane Packer write that the universal supply of money is infinite, and that it is within every human being's reach to live with enough food, shelter, warmth and clothing.

Changing your beliefs about the scarcity of money opens you to limitless financial possibilities. There's enough pizza to go around.

2. I will let go and trust the universe.

You are doing the work you love. You have developed a sound business plan. You are following the *10 Commandments of Small-Business Success.*

Have faith this whole crazy thing called life will work out, and quit worrying about it.

Most small businesses struggle in the beginning. Owners carry the feeling of scarcity–caused by that struggle and reinforced by their past beliefs–over to times that are prosperous. Trained to work long, hard hours, these entrepreneurs don't see that now prosperity is theirs. The fear remains.

Ironically, the fear of losing money in your business can cause it to happen. Gandhi said, "All fear is a sign of want of faith."

Entrepreneurs must, after sowing the seeds of prosperity, have faith the seeds will come to fruition–and enjoy the harvest when they do. Owners can control where they plant the seeds, and how much they fertilize and water them, but cannot control the sun, rain or storms. It takes faith.

Whatever happens in your business or life, you must believe it happens for a reason, and that it serves a greater purpose. It's often difficult to believe that's true when the worst happens, but how many times have we seen wonderful things happen after life has kicked us square on the behind? We'll discuss this more in The Tenth Commandment.

3. I realize there is a time for planting and a time for harvest.

To create money, you must realize all businesses go through cycles. Just as Egypt suffered through seven years of plenty and seven years of famine in the Bible story in Genesis, businesses also go through economic ups and downs. It is important to expect these cycles and be prepared for them.

When sales are sluggish, use that time to contact old customers as well as find new ones. Study your competition and learn from their mistakes. Train employees and build a strong team feeling. If you need to cut expenses, such as travel budgets, discuss this with your employees and get feedback. Communicate to them that business cycles are natural and you still believe in the prosperity of your company. Do what you don't have time to do when sales are explosive. Continue to believe.

Many business owners fail because they overexpand in times of plenty and have too much overhead in lean times. Let your business grow slowly but steadily.

It isn't going to rain $100 bills every day.

In lean times, cut back and use the opportunity to make internal improvements. My law practice is always dead in February. The first year, I worried the phone was broken, and the phone company patiently answered my repeated inquiries. Finally, March came and the phone rang off the hook. I learned to use February to work on office procedures and refine the year's business plan. I soon looked forward to the month-long slowdown for business improvements we did not have time for the rest of the year. The slow cycle became vital to my business.

4. I am responsible for creating my abundance.

While it's certainly fine to believe you are guided by a higher power, you must behave as if you are responsible for creating wealth. The buck stops here. Don't blame your spouse, your parents, the government, your competition, the Federal Reserve, your neighbor, your seventh-grade teacher or anyone else for a failure to create money. No, it isn't always your fault, but you must believe it is up to you.

Seizing prosperity means you must believe in your ability to be prosperous during periods of economic decline. A small company's survival depends on believing that economic downturns reveal unexpected opportunities, because small businesses can adjust to shifting market conditions more quickly than large enterprises. When a market goes sour, competition flees, leaving the survivors a larger market share. This is most evident in businesses that, by their nature, are influenced by outside factors.

For example, when home interest rates are low, home sales prosper and many new real-estate businesses open. When interest rates rise, as they always do, companies close their doors. If you are a broker and stick it out, you have less competition and a larger share of the market. Also, you are establishing longevity for your company and building a solid client base.

Business cycles affect you only to the extent that you let them. If you believe your business is prosperous, you will look within yourself for guidance through hard times and find ways to survive until times get better.

5. I will focus on what I want financially.

Studies have shown that a police squad car pulled over on the side of the road with its blue lights flashing is many times more likely to be hit by a passing car than a police car with its emergency lights turned off.

Sounds silly, doesn't it? How could someone see a police car with flashing lights and still be stupid enough to run into it?

It's the bug-to-the-light syndrome: You get what you focus on.

Too many people spend their time focusing on what they don't want instead of what they want. "I don't want to get sick." They get sick. "I don't want to be broke." Soon, they're broke. Their car slides on ice toward a wall–instead of focusing on where they want to go, they focus on not hitting the wall. Smack.

Focus your attention and energies on what you want financially. Pay special attention to what you say about money, both in your head and to others.

6. I believe money is neither good nor bad.

Money is paper or coin. It is simply a man-made medium of exchange. There is nothing inherently wonderful or evil about it.

Bad feelings about money exist because of experiences associated with it, as shown by what happened in my college days. To live a happy life and put money in the right light, you need to get past feelings like this. If I had not examined my experiences with money, I would have been in for a lifelong financial nightmare.

One of the greatest misquotes of all time is that "money is the root of all evil." The Bible tells us that the *love* of money is the root of all evil.

Money can do wonderful things. It can feed, clothe and shelter the hungry. It can give you peace of mind. It can give you time. It should not be the ultimate goal, but simply a piece of the puzzle. Looking at money in the wrong light also has started wars, caused hard feelings and murders, and created a lot of stress.

Money is a tool to get what you want in life, and to help others. Do you have money in perspective?

7. I believe I deserve financial security.

You'd be surprised how many business owners don't believe in their hearts that they deserve wealth and prosperity.

They believe they're not good enough, not smart enough, not beautiful enough. "Others deserve it, not me." Oftentimes, these are beliefs they developed during childhood and never got over.

You can always find a reason not to be successful. Stop looking for one.

You deserve to be prosperous, and you have everything you need to begin creating money. Today. But you need to believe in your heart that you deserve a prosperous life. And, you deserve it as much as anyone.

There's a great difference between humility, which every successful person must have, and a self-image problem. When you start to succeed, thank others and the universe for helping you. No one does it alone. But you will not succeed unless you believe you deserve it; even if you show signs of success, you'll find one way or another to sabotage it.

8. I must see financial success in my mind before I can achieve it.

You have to visualize your success before you can grasp it. Become a success in your head long before your financial gains show up on paper.

Be specific about what success means to you–both in life and in terms of financial security.

I recently heard a man tell a story about how he told friends he was going to come to America from the Philippines and become a millionaire. Sure enough, he did it! Unfortunately, he became a millionaire not in U.S. dollars, but in Filipino pesos. He never made the distinction. He now has refined his goals and sees himself every day as an American millionaire. I have no doubt he'll get there in the next few years. He sure believes he will!

The power of repetition is incredible when it comes to visualizing financial success. Determine what you want, and repeat it in your head–morning, noon and night. See yourself meeting your financial goals. What will you do for your spouse? Yourself? Your children? Others?

Remember when you were a kid and there was something you wanted? It was all you could think about! As an adult, you have to develop that same attitude toward prosperity. Think of what you want financially–see it, feel it, touch it, smell it. Place pictures of it up on the wall. Keep it in front of you at all times.

9. I will create money by giving money away.

It might sound contrary, but it works. You cannot create true abundance unless you give money away.

When you give without expecting anything in return, the universe has a strange way of bringing money back to you many times over.

Give money away because it is the right thing to do, not because it's a tactic.

Many companies even work charity into the elaboration of their mission statements. Giving money away is part of the business plan!

It's up to you where you tithe, but find good causes and support them. Set aside a certain portion of income to help others. The choices are infinite. Save the ocean. Help an employee or friend who's going through hard times. Give to charities or churches. Give to a homeless shelter. Share whatever you can with those who are less fortunate.

One of the most wonderful things you can do in addition to giving money is to give of your time. Set aside a few hours regularly to give to needy local causes.

Giving to worthy causes also helps free people from unhealthy attachments to money. Remember, money is currency, and currency should flow!

I even know of one woman who pulls a dollar out of her purse every day and drops it on the ground on her way to work. Why in the world would she do that? She said it helps her keep money in perspective, and it brightens a stranger's day. You can't buy much more than that for a buck!

Creating money by giving it away also means you are always honorable in your business dealings, and that you share your financial success with employees. If you are a good person to do business with, companies will go out of their way to work with you. If you are a generous employer in prosperous times, more employees will work harder to please you, and will be more likely to stick by you during downturns in your business.

Remember, everyone is unique and has a special contribution to make. If you follow The First Commandment and specialize in what you know and love, you will attract prosperity. You will feel happy and fulfilled in your work, and this joy will spill over into your business. If you honor and develop your special skills and talents, you will feel alive and prosperous. Know that there is an unlimited supply of prosperity in the world, and, if you visualize prosperity in your life daily, you will have it.

Visualize it. Breathe it in. Believe me, it does work.

I advocate using the analytical part of your brain to analyze your business situation and decide how you can spend less and earn more. Prepare a sound business plan. Then, have faith, and use the creative part of your brain to attract money into your life. Don't neglect this half–a business owner needs both.

Exercise One

Spend quiet time thinking about what money means to you. How much do you want to have? Why do you want to have this amount? What would having this amount of money mean to you? What old beliefs could you toss out and what new beliefs could you adopt that will make you more prosperous? What does true prosperity mean to you, beyond money?

Exercise Two

Create A Money Tree

To be successful, you must believe you can be successful. Otherwise, you are like the skier careening down the snowy mountain thinking, "I'm going to crash; I'm going to fall; I'll never make it." If he holds this thought, no matter how many lessons he's had, he will crash. The fear of crashing keeps the skier stiff and off balance; if the skier were relaxed and confident, he would naturally make the necessary body adjustments to stay balanced. So, when you feel like the out-of-control skier, regain your balance and your faith by learning to create money in your life. Grow a money tree.

Here's how:

1. Relax in a comfortable chair.
2. Close your eyes and take nine slow, deep breaths.
3. Clear your mind.

4. Visualize a huge tree, with limbs full of bright green dollar bills–with a shining light around it.

5. See on the tree the number of dollars you wish to create.

6. Believe you can create it! You might want to start small so you will believe your goal is attainable.

7. Take several deep breaths and every time you do, see all the money you want coming to you with each breath. Keep doing this until you believe it. You'll feel the energy click when it happens. Feel the money covering you. Play in it, roll in it as you would in a huge pile of leaves.

8. Repeat steps 1-7 daily throughout the month. Whenever you are feeling broke and have thoughts of scarcity, replace those thoughts with a picture of the money tree and feelings of wealth.

9. Do not limit ways the money can come to you–it comes in many unexpected forms when you open your mind.

10. Make sure you write me about your experience after it works! Remember, it takes energy, concentration and the belief you can do it to make this exercise a success.

The Seventh Commandment

Seek Silence in Chaos

"I never thought other than that God is that great absence in our lives, the empty silence within, the peace where we go seeking not in hope to arrive or find."

—Irene Thomas, *Via Negativa*

"We need to find God, and he can not be found in noise and restlessness. God is the friend of silence. We need silence to be able to touch souls."

—Mother Teresa, *A Gift for God*

I had been toying with different titles for this chapter when life gave me the answer.

My two sons were back. One had just graduated from college and moved home temporarily to find a job. The other was packing to leave for college. Every room in my house was as crowded as a fraternity house party–boxes, beds, furniture, friends, plates, pans, stereos and so forth. With one son rebuilding his Jeep for the trip to Colorado, the garage was a mess. The driveway, packed with friends' Jeeps, resembled an Army parking lot. The refrigerator, which I refilled daily, magically emptied every night.

I was bringing home work every evening from my law practice, and my deadline for turning in the final rewrite of this manuscript was looming. I felt out of control. My business and personal lives were in chaos.

At that instant, a strong voice inside my head repeated, "Seek silence in chaos."

I dropped everything, jumped in my car and drove to a wooded park nearby. I plopped down under a towering old oak tree and cleared my head. I listened to the silence. My focus returned. I returned home an hour later to finish some paperwork, then enjoyed a great night of writing. What started as a disaster ended as a satisfying, profitable day.

Find Your Inner Voice ... and Listen

For entrepreneurs, seeking silence and listening to what it tells you is as important as listening to your rational business mind. Amid the chaos of entrepreneurial life, there are times when you must toss everything aside and listen to that voice of wisdom inside your head. You might call it your inner voice, the voice of God, your intuition, your gut feeling, spiritual guidance, a hunch, an educated guess, special insight, an impulse or seat-of-your-pants management. No matter what you believe it is, you must believe it is important to your success.

Companies are realizing the importance of teaching their employees to follow their instincts and hunches. Hundreds of business consultants are teaching the importance of intuition, which is defined as knowledge that comes to a person without any conscious remembrance or reason. It is information from other than the normal, rational mind.

Business owners who mix intuition with their rational processes have an incredible edge in business. These entrepreneurs use the analytical part of the brain to handle the daily business details. Unfortunately, most entrepreneurs become overloaded with information, and decision-making grows tedious. This is when wise entrepreneurs shift mental gears to make use of the listening, creative and spiritual parts of the brain.

In this state of mind, we are no longer actively thinking. The mental chatter in our head ceases and we have access to an awareness level that can guide us through difficult times and help us make major decisions. In times of silence, we can become aware of information that is not normally accessible to us.

All new inventions started as ideas. An inventor visualizes what he wants, then uses his analytical knowledge to achieve it. A writer dreams the plot for a story, then uses the rational mind to fashion a workable outline in which to unfold the story. Albert Einstein spoke often about how using intuition helped him develop theories. An entrepreneur dreams of a new market for his product, then takes his dream to work and analyzes the economic costs and benefits. All are examples of blending intuition with the rational mind.

In my law practice and life, I have always sought guidance from my inner voice, which I believe is guidance from God but you might see in a different light. Almost all of my successful clients say they rely on an inner voice of some sort to guide them.

Jeff Andrews owns a successful restaurant chain. Restaurants are risky endeavors that are subject to high failure rates. Yet, Jeff has succeeded for a quarter century.

He told me:

"I clear my mind daily by running three miles. While running alone, new solutions for problems and new ideas pop into my head. I take these ideas back to my business."

Entrepreneur Robert Winslow takes a four-day weekend each month to go to a monastery and reflect.

"I have found the value of silence in my chaotic world," Winslow said. "I walk around in the beautiful woods surrounding the monastery and listen to the silence. At first it was hard–I felt jumpy and my mind constantly chattered to me, but I kept returning. Now, I love coming here. My mind slows down as soon as I begin the drive into the mountains.

On Monday, I return to work refreshed, with new ideas and a new outlook.

"Taking time away has given me more time in my life, because I solve problems faster. At first, my family was skeptical that this would help me. Now, they see the change, and I actually have more time with them because I solve problems quickly and work more efficiently. It helps me focus and greatly assists me in decision making."

Carol took a meditation course at a community college to help her deal with the chaotic pace of her advertising agency.

"Through practicing meditation only 15 minutes each morning, I am more aware of my intuitional guidance," Carol said. "It has helped me greatly, by accomplishing difficult (tasks) and attaining business goals. By letting go of the struggle to control my mind, I have learned that it leads me where I want to go."

More Than One Way to Think

In *Think and Grow Rich*, Napoleon Hill calls this the sixth sense, the "receiving set" through which ideas and plans flash in the mind. He likens this sense to a guardian angel who leads and protects you.

Psychologist Carl Jung included intuition as one of four major faculties of the psyche, along with thinking, feeling and sensation.

Penney Pierce, in *The Intuitional Way*, states that intuition is not the opposite of logic, but intuition comes through visions, dreams, fantasies, voices, vibrations, feelings and hunches in your head. It can come through any of the senses.

Suzi Daggett conducts workshops on using the intuitional process in the workplace. Her California company, Insight, teaches entrepreneurs to recognize their inner knowledge and blend it with the outer deductions and data to arrive at decisions.

"Intuitive information is whole-picture processing, rather than bits and pieces of data, such as we use when we think logically," Daggett said. "Sometimes an intuitive thought will seem bizarre or not make sense until after an incident, and then, 'A-ha!,' it all falls into place."

Daggett explained that many small-business owners use intuition daily, because they have little time to process all the data necessary to make decisions. This is especially true in today's fast-paced, fast-changing business world.

Business people "will most readily admit that time and knowledge constraints require them to use something other than intellect or logic for decision making," she said. "They rely on their gut or intuition for quick, reliable decisions. If they make a mistake by following their hunch, they will regroup and start again, learning from the experience rather than feeling they have erred. This is the difference between someone who uses their inner sense for moving forward in business and one who is fearful of every decision ever made."

One of Daggett's workshop participants shared this story:

Tammy was interviewing people for a position as chef. One prospect looked, acted and talked like the outstanding chef his resume boasted he was. She needed to fill the position quickly, so she hired him on the spot–even though a voice inside her insisted, "Do not hire this man!" Tammy had never heard a voice like that before, and she didn't know what to do.

The chef worked at her restaurant for four months. Four agonizing months. His cooking was lousy, and his attitude destroyed staff morale. The cost of hiring and firing him was outstanding. Next time, Tammy will listen carefully to her inner voice. Had she listened the first time, she would have saved money, time and her restaurant's reputation.

Ignoring Intuition

President Woodrow Wilson said, "One cool judgment is worth a thousand hasty counsels. The thing to do is supply light, not heat." Certain times, people ignore their intuition, even when the message is clear. This can happen for a number of reasons:

• Some are afraid of intuition, thinking it will lead them down a frightful, freaky, ghost-filled path. They are more comfortable with reason and facts.

• Sometimes, we don't like what our intuition tells us, and we kill the messenger. Your spouse tells you he is late because he had to work, but your intuition tells you he is not telling the truth. Your intuition tells you to get out of a certain business, but you ignore the warnings because you want to avoid the upheaval that will cause.

• Some don't believe intuition exists.

Intuition *does* exist, it is important, and you, as a small-business owner, had better not ignore it.

How, in a business, can you use it?

• An intuitive flash guided a businessperson to purchase more of a certain item, just before the price increased;

• Intuition told one businessman to avoid signing a contract to extend his lease. Two days later, he had a chance to move to a better location;

• Intuition helps me avoid taking clients who later prove dishonest;

• Intuition will help you take any leap of faith, to make a decision without having every fact;

• Intuition can help you solve many business problems instantly once you stop agonizing about them.

Learning to Use Intuition

We all have an inner voice, but some of us have never listened to it, while others stopped calling upon it years ago. The good news is, it never goes away. Intuition is waiting in the wings, willing and able to be your friend and confidant, regardless of how you treated it in the past. So, how do we discover or rediscover intuition?

Every person will have a different way of getting in touch with his inner voice. But the one element common to most people is silence. While the inner voice occasionally busts through the brick wall of life's noise and delivers an unsolicited opinion, it more often requires you to take an active role to be silent and seek its insight.

To clearly access intuition, your body must be healthy. Eat right. Exercise regularly. Intuition is often impossible to hear through alcohol or other drugs, which usually allow us to access only our emotional voices. Have you ever written someone a letter when you were drinking margaritas, then read it the next day and said, "Thank goodness I did not mail that!"?

You also need to trust both yourself and the universe to tune in to your intuition. If you don't have faith in both yourself and the big picture in life, you won't get the most out of this wonderful part of the mind.

The first step toward accessing your intuition is to silence the external world. Go somewhere where you won't be bothered, such as a quiet room where you can lock the door, or a park, or the woods. No phone, no kids, no employees–just you and your inner voice.

Next, you must silence the internal world. The constant chatter in your head is more often a nosy neighbor than your intuition, and you need to shut it up. You spend all day listening to internal chatter, and you need to be able to tune it out at times such as these.

If you are having a hard time stopping the chatter, you might want to imagine yourself turning the volume knob on this noise to "off," or pushing the sound away into the distance. (This also can be helpful if you are having trouble sleeping–the chatter sometimes is the cause, and learning to turn it off can help you sleep.) Strong emotional feelings also must go with the chatter, as these will skew the results. You must be relaxed.

Once you have internal and external silence, you should ask your inner voice for guidance in whatever areas you need help in. The answers might not appear in the form you are expecting, or at that very moment, so you need to be aware of the ways in which intuition can speak to you. Answers can come to you in pictures, words you see, words you hear, sounds, feelings, impressions.

Each person experiences intuition differently. You need to learn your intuition's unique language. One of your senses, be it hearing, sight, smell, taste or touch, is your predominant sensory antenna to the world. The best way to start getting in touch with your intuition is to figure out which sense is strongest to you. What do you first notice when you enter a room? Colors? Smells? Sounds? Feelings?

I have always used my sense of smell, much to the horror of my parents, to determine if I wanted to eat something. It was not good Southern manners in Georgia to smell the food at a dinner party. I also respond to people by sense of smell. I'm not speaking of an obvious odor, but my nose sends me subtle messages. When I first meet someone, my nose is the first to react, then I see pictures and have feelings about that person. I have found that sense of smell is predominant when my intuition speaks to me.

If you are more visual, your intuition might come as words or pictures in your mind. If you are more auditory, you might hear sounds or voices. If you are more feeling, or kinesthetic, you might feel what you should do.

You also can try to access your intuition by writing. Relax, take several deep breaths, clear your mind and let your pen write for 10 or 15 minutes while you turn off your editor. Don't even wonder if what you are writing makes sense.

Then, read what you've written–you might be surprised at what is there.

Flashes of Inspiration

Although intuition is harder to access when you're not amid internal and external peace, it sometimes speaks to you during periods when you let your conscious guard down–such as during exercise, while driving or when you're in the shower–or during a repetitive, mindless activity such as washing the car or cutting the lawn. It's a good idea to keep a pen and paper nearby at all times to write thoughts that flash in your mind.

Answers also can come in dreams. In my dreams, I sometimes watch detailed conversations between people. In a day or two, the same conversation will occur in my office. It's like watching a TV show repeat! Be careful with dreams, however, as you need to differentiate between intuitive messages and mind junk. There's a mix of both in our dreams.

The challenge with intuition is that the timing of the message isn't always according to your clock, and you can't always be sure the message you're hearing is true intuition and not the result of emotions. You need to learn to trust your inner voice, but be able to differentiate between it and every emotional thought that rolls through your head. It takes time and practice.

In addition, if you haven't relied on intuition much, it's still there, but it might take some time for it to grow to being highly reliable. What happens when you don't use one of your muscles? As the saying goes, if you don't use it, you lose it. The more you exercise your intuition, the more valuable a tool it will become in your business and personal life.

How do you know when something is an intuitive flash, as opposed to an emotional reaction? I use "The Rule of Threes." If I get a strong impulse to act, and am not sure whether it is intuitive or emotional, I wait until the impulse or message occurs three times before I respond.

Sometimes, your intuition will concur with the facts. But when there's a clear contradiction, it's especially important to keep revisiting the question with your inner voice until you're sure the message is clear. When logic and intuition smack head-to-head, I trust my intuition, and find that this decision is usually correct.

But How Can I, the Superentrepreneur, Find Time to Seek Silence in Chaos?

I know, I know ... there just aren't enough hours in the day. But you need to make time for both relaxation and meditation. In fact, you must do so if you want to access your intuition and be successful. It's good for your mental and physical health, it's good for your family, and it's good for your business.

The following tips to help entrepreneurs get away are adapted from *The Home Team: How to Live, Love and Work at Home* (Bookhome Publishing) by Scott Gregory and Shirley Siluk Gregory:

• **The spontaneous break.** Work is slow and the weather is balmy, so you decide to take off early to lie in the sun in your backyard. Or, 101 little frustrations through the day have chipped away at your sanity, and you need to get out of the office and go for a walk. Do it. These little breathers don't have to take a lot of time–even an hour can work wonders when you're stressed–but they can act as a much-needed escape valve when business pressures become overwhelming.

• **The scheduled breather.** Again, these interludes don't have to eat big holes into your work time. Schedule 15 minutes every morning to relax and think. Get to the office ahead of your employees. Plan a lunchtime break to try that new restaurant you have been hearing so many good things about. Or, set aside time one afternoon to see the latest release at the movie theater–before the kids get out of school and way before the nighttime date crowd packs the house. Taken regularly, these little interruptions are an important way to preserve your mental health by getting you away before your office begins feeling like a sweat shop.

• **The short getaway.** Wednesday's forecast is hot and sunny, while the weekend promises to be cool and soggy. So, why not plan a mid-week day off to enjoy the weather, and use Saturday as your regular workday instead? It's amazing how refreshed you can feel after one day in a different and work-free environment. And breaking up the week into two- or three-day segments also makes work go a lot easier.

• **The weekend.** For business owners, this can be the hardest break of all to take regularly. Without occasional weekend breathers, though, it doesn't take long to feel as if you never can get away from your work ... and to end up resenting it. You might even find yourself envying friends who work 9-to-5 corporate jobs Monday through Friday, and that's not a feeling you want. Do yourself a favor: set aside at least one weekend a month to play and reflect.

• **The full-fledged vacation.** A magazine article for entre-preneurs once described the vacation as a sign you were "making it." Really, though, it's more an indication of good long-term planning, which certainly is the kind of thing that leads to success. A vacation itself is no great accomplish-ment: there are plenty of teenagers working full-time, semi-skilled jobs who can take a week off once they have put in enough time. Arranging your work schedule, preparing clients, budgeting extra money to escape your business for a while: those are the real signs you're "making it."

A vacation doesn't have to mean the stereotypical week at the Grand Canyon or in Orlando. You might prefer spend-ing the time sprucing up your garden during the day and experimenting with new recipes on the backyard grill every evening. Your mind needs an extended rest at least a couple times a year.

Whatever type of respite you prefer, it's critical to schedule time for yourself. It's vital that–even on the most pressure-packed and crisis-filled days–you can look at your calendar and know there's a moment or two coming up that will allow you to relax, escape and think. No one should take pride in laboring non-stop for months or years without a break.

Do you ever find yourself saying, "There's no way I can ever get away"? You can sometimes find yourself facing a problem without an apparent solution because all the little things that could have helped you were neglected in the past. A business can be filled with such traps ... unless you have prepared. When it comes to being able to take a break, make sure you have taken steps along the way that can set you free. Here are a few to consider:

• **Voice mail/answering machine/answering service.** Unless your business doesn't depend a bit on telephone calls, you're attempting the impossible by working without one of these. You also need a willingness to ignore the telephone when you're taking a break; if you're in the middle of some much-needed free time, feeling the need to answer every call will frustrate you more than not having a breather to begin with. If your business depends on orders, it's a good idea to have a live voice on the line during business hours, so an answering service could be a must. Otherwise, don't fear voice mail. If the call is important, the caller will leave a message.

• **A planning calendar.** You don't have to rigidly pencil in work from 9 a.m. to 6 p.m. every weekday, with a half-hour for lunch. But you should have a fairly clear idea of what you need to do every day and how long each job will take. That accomplished, you will have a better idea of where the best possibilities lie for free hours and days–and you can plan them. Then, you just need the resolve to stick to your schedule. Only real emergencies should interfere. Don't waste your days putting out every tiny fire someone else sets. You control your calendar. Sunday night is the perfect time to sit down and plan the week, as your focus is past the weekend and on the week ahead.

• **A reasonably organized office.** You don't have to be the King or Queen of Neat. But if you can tell with not much more than a glance how much work has come in and how much needs to go out, you will have a better gauge of what your day and week will look like–and where you might have time for a break.

• **Delegation skills.** People who take pride in their work–especially if they are self-employed–tend to think they need to do it all. After all, it's their venture, their name on the business cards, their reputation. Realizing they can't do everything, smart business owners make the most of their employees' talents, as well as form ongoing and occasional partnerships with talented folks at other companies. You can contract with these people to handle tasks when you are overwhelmed or need to get away, or they can handle parts of the job you might not be as good at so you can focus your talents on other aspects of your business.

• **An ability to say no.** Say it five times now–no, no, no, no, no. A simple two letters, but it certainly is one of the toughest words in the English language. If it were easy to say, you wouldn't have telemarketers calling you every 30 minutes, and you wouldn't have purchased that rustproofing for your new car. Don't make a habit of trying to be Superman, Superwoman or Supercouple. Yes, you need to work to pay the bills, but if you overload yourself with more projects than you can humanly handle, you will end up frazzled, sad and–more than likely–unable to finish all your work satisfactorily. This will make your clients teary-eyed, too, before they go looking for someone else to handle the next job. Be realistic about your work, even if it means turning down an occasional project.

Exercise

Take out your planning calendar now and schedule at least 15 minutes of quiet time each day for the next week. Make this a daily habit. Within the next three months, set aside two or three days consecutive days during which you commit to doing nothing but relaxing and reflecting.

The Eighth Commandment

Form a Firm Foundation

I asked Bill, who sat across from me in my office, about the business structure of his computer service enterprise.

"Oh, I did it right ... it's incorporated," he said.

I asked why.

"I have no idea," Bill said with a surprised shrug. "My friend said do it, so I told my lawyer to do it. So, he incorporated me."

"How long ago?"

"About three years."

"Do you have corporate by-laws? Have you had corporate meetings or minutes, or issued stock?"

"No," said Bill, leaning forward, looking puzzled and concerned. "Is all of that necessary?"

In some states, Bill would not be incorporated because he has not completed all the requirements necessary to form and maintain a legal corporation. Bill's business did not have a firm foundation.

One doctor I know joined in a general partnership with five of his colleagues to buy a hospital. Six doctors and $3 million in debt, so that's a $500,000 debt each, right?

Wrong!

The doctors thought it worked that way until one doctor couldn't pay his share of the debt, then another. In a partnership, when one can't pay, the responsibility falls to the others. The last guy trying to hold out against bankruptcy ended up owing all $3 million.

The doctors had no idea why they bought the hospital in a general partnership. It was, simply, simpler. Everyone said he would pay his portion. Had the doctors owned shares in a corporation and one could not pay, the remaining doctors would have had better legal protection, and we might not be looking at six bankruptcies.

The legal organization of your business depends on what goals you want to achieve. Many would-be entrepreneurs come to see me after they have mailed the Lawyer-In-A-Box, Do-It-Yourself Corporate Kit. Incorporating is not the automatic thing to do. Choosing a business structure requires a detailed analysis of many legal, economic and psychological factors. You can't make a blanket statement that any one structure is better than another, and you shouldn't choose a structure based on what someone else has done.

There are three main types of business ownership used in the United States: sole proprietorships, general and limited partnerships, and corporations.

The form of legal organization you require depends on the type of business you own, the protection from liability you need, tax issues, the size of your business, the number of investors, the amount of paperwork you're willing to do, how you intend to raise capital, future needs and an array of laws or regulations that affect your type of business.

Let's look at each structure:

Sole Proprietorships

Two people work for Mac's Mobile Car Wash—Mac and his employee, Dave. Mac has decided to operate his business as a sole proprietorship, the most common business structure in America.

Sole proprietorships are owned and run by one individual, or a husband and wife. The owner controls the business, receives all the profits and is responsible for all losses. He has no shield to protect his personal assets from business debt.

The advantage–and this is why it is the most popular–is that this business type is quickly and inexpensively formed. You can file an assumed name certificate and start doing business immediately (although you might have to obtain some licenses, depending on where you live and what you do). Legal fees and accounting costs are minimal. Mac will have a D.B.A.–meaning he is "doing business as" Mac's Mobile Car Wash.

The disadvantages are many in times of trouble. If the business falls into financial hot water, the owner's assets are automatically thrown into the pot and can be seized by creditors. There also is no protection from liability caused by employees' acts. For example, if Dave accidentally washes someone's car with paint remover, Mac could get sued and lose his business and personal assets subject to a creditor's levy, unless state law protects such personal items (even then, the protection is usually minimal).

With our litigious society and economic ups and downs, many entrepreneurs are looking to other legal structures that provide better protection. Often, a business will start as a sole proprietorship and change legal form after it grows.

Sole Proprietorship

Advantages

1. Easy to start—find a place and open the doors.
2. Low cost, minimum start up costs and legal fees.

Disadvantages

1. If owner dies, the business may die.
2. Might be hard to finance; investors might not be interested because they will not own part of the business.

3. Owner has total authority	3. Unlimited liability of the owner for business debts.
4. The owners get all the profits.	4. Hard to keep business, personal affairs separate.

Corporations

Mac could incorporate his business. Then, he would do business as Mac's Mobile Car Wash Inc. The biggest difference would be, in his case, liability protection. If Dave accidentally put paint remover on someone's car, the customer could not sue Mac–only his corporation. The corporate shield would protect him.

For this discussion, we'll refer to corporations as if they are privately owned, and assume the bulk of the stock is owned by people who take an active role in running the business.

There are other advantages to corporate ownership. You can raise funds through sale of stock, if you can find someone to buy it. And, stockholders have little or no liability for the debts of the corporation. If the corporation files bankruptcy, the stockholders only lose their stock–they don't have to pay the corporate debts.

However, most major lending institutions will not lend money to a small-business corporation without the major stockholders personally guaranteeing the loan.

Despite personal guaranty requirements, a corporation still might have many advantages for you, such as limiting liability in the case of defective products, frivolous lawsuits, employee negligence and debt exposure. There also is the ease of changing of corporation ownership–when one of the stockholders dies, the corporation does not. The stock of the deceased owner may be sold, or passed on to the heirs.

Administrative costs for a corporation are high, however, both in terms of what must be spent to pay professionals to start the corporation as well as ensure all paperwork requirements are met. The administrative requirements will cut into an owner's time, especially in a small shop. And you can't cut corners here: attorneys have successfully gone to court and attacked corporations as shams because they did not follow proper procedures, and have cut through the corporate shield to get at an owner's personal assets.

Corporations have more tax options than the other structures, but corporations usually pay higher state taxes and owners often find themselves victims of double taxation.

An alternative that is growing in popularity is the Subchapter S-Corporation. This is not a different form of ownership from the regular C-Corporation discussed above; it is simply an election to have the tax attributes, incomes and losses of the corporation flow through to the owners.

Corporation

Advantages
1. Can sell shares to raise money.

2. Liability of shareholders is limited.
3. Easy to transfer ownership.

Disadvantages
1. Might have tax disadvantages
2. Expensive to start and and maintain.
3. Must keep corporate books and records.
4. Decisions must be made as set out in bylaws.

Partnerships

When two or more people come together and agree to share in the profits and losses of a business, you have a partnership. A general partnership does not bear the same tax burdens as a corporation; profits or losses are simply passed through to an individual's personal income tax return, and a financial information report is filed with the government.

One of the frequent problems with this form of ownership is the belief that the partners are liable only for their percentage of ownership share of the partnership's debt.

This is a misconception, as shown by the earlier case with the doctors. With a general partnership or joint venture, all partners are "jointly and severally liable" for the corporate debts. Thus, if one partner does not pay his share, the other partner has to take up the slack. One falls, all fall.

A Tale of Two Carpet Cleaners

Frank owned a successful carpet-cleaning company. Chris was his only competition. So Frank and Chris decided, if they joined together, they could control the market and make more money. They developed a general partnership agreement from a computer form because it was fast, easy and inexpensive. Chris failed to tell Frank he had not paid his old company's bills and taxes, and creditors came after the new, joint company and levied on the assets.

In a partnership, all partners also are legally bound to the actions another partner might take. For example, if one partner inks a new deal on behalf of the partnership, all partners are bound to it, even if they weren't consulted beforehand.

As is the case with sole proprietorships, personal assets are at risk, unless there are protections under state law.

Although you can legally have a partnership without a written agreement, you should have everything in writing. Beyond the agreement, startup paperwork is minimal, about the same as forming a sole proprietorship. Income tax paperwork is a bit more complex.

One vital part the partnership agreement should cover is what happens if one partner wants out or dies. In about half the states, the partnership is dissolved and assets are liquidated when a partner leaves or dies unless options are spelled out in the agreement.

As a partner, you are entitled to all information about the partnership. You also are bound to fairness and loyalty to your partners in financial matters, meaning you could be in for legal trouble if you do anything unethical or undermining to the partnership.

Another form of partnership is a limited partnership, which is usually formed as a fund-raising mechanism for real-estate investment. In a limited partnership, you have one or more general partners who share responsibilities as with a general partnership. But the limited partners rarely take part in the management of the business, and they do not share personal liability for the partnership's debts or judgments. There also are tax benefits for limited partners.

Yet another type of partnership, often confused with a limited partnership, is a limited liability partnership, or LLP. This business structure, which is growing increasingly popular, is similar to a general partnership, but you wouldn't be personally liable for the negligent acts of other partners. It offers the flexibility of a partnership with the liability protection of a corporation.

General Partnership

Advantages	*Disadvantages*
1. Easy to start.	1.Unlimited liability.
2. More people to raise money and support loans.	2. Each is responsible for all of the debt.
3. Someone to help out and share ideas; two heads might be better than one.	3. Might be difficult to agree with partner; difficult to dissolve unless both agree.
	4. Death or bankruptcy of one partner endangers the business.

Contracts

Another way to form a firm foundation is to be sure all deals between yourself and others are clear and in writing.

A contract is an agreement between two or more parties spelling out their promises. Although oral agreements are binding in many cases, they're almost impossible to prove in a court of law, and some types are invalid under state law. So, have everything in writing.

When a business is starting, everyone is optimistic and agreeable. You will hear, "We trust each other. We don't need to write that down." Or, "We'll worry about that later." Beware: the handshake days are gone.

A contract should clearly describe each party's rights and responsibilities, plus set out what remedies are available if any party breaches the agreement. Negotiate your contracts carefully. Put aside personal feelings, both good and bad, and negotiate at arm's length as if the party were a stranger.

The period of negotiation is the time to come to agreement on all possible differences and to agree on remedies and damages if a breach occurs. Because most contract negotiations occur at the beginning of a business relationship, many people do not feel comfortable negotiating and establishing clear guidelines for fear it will damage the relationship. They labor under a romantic notion that any disagreement in the future can be amicably worked out. Hey, we're all fair and rational human beings, right?

Nothing is further from the truth. When a dispute occurs, emotions enter the picture, and memories of the terms of an agreement will differ radically. You often will find yourself feeling as if you're speaking to someone different from the person you made the deal with. You won't believe the spin some folks will put on what you know to be the truth!

Many people fear contracts because most documents they see contain extensive legalese. So, they avoid contracts altogether, which is a huge mistake.

Many agreements require simply a few sentences, written in clear English. For a contract to be legal, the participants must be in agreement–one party has made an offer and another has accepted–and something of value must be exchanged (such as goods, services, cash or promises to deliver these).

It's vital to have deals in writing because the element of acceptance can be in dispute. For example, let's say you want to purchase 25 copies of this book from me, and I say that the price is $300. This is my offer. If you tell me to go ahead and send them, we have a contract. But if you don't respond, or you say you aren't sure, or if you make a counteroffer of $250, there's no deal yet under the law.

I can revoke my offer any time before acceptance. But once you accept the offer, it's a binding agreement. I can't change my mind. The exception is if both of us agree the offer remains open for a set period of time.

If you made the counteroffer of $250, I can accept it, decline it, or make a counteroffer of my own. If I accept it, the deal is made. If I make a counteroffer of $275, the ball is back in your court.

Once the terms are agreed on, fax or mail a written summary and get it signed!

The exchange of value portion, known as "consideration," ensures each party is getting something in the deal. For example, say I promise to come over Saturday and mow your lawn. If I don't show up, you probably aren't going to invite me to the Sunday cookout, but there isn't anything you can do legally. However, if I promise to mow your lawn Saturday in exchange for you driving me to the mall on Wednesday, we have a contract!

You certainly can't go running to your attorney for every single deal you make in your business life, but you should have an attorney develop, or at least review, all documents you consider vital to your business. You'll have to decide on a case-by-case basis but, when in doubt, be safe. When you make the decision not to use an attorney for any deal, be sure all terms are in writing! The surest way to hurt a personal or business relationship is to make an oral agreement in good faith, then run head-on into a disagreement later. Putting terms in writing shows you respect the other party and wish to develop a mutually satisfactory relationship.

If your business is owned by more than one person, one contract you must have, and your attorney must review, is a buy-sell agreement. It might be tomorrow, it might be 50 years from now, but sooner or later, one or more of the owners will want out of the business.

This can happen for a multitude of reasons: an owner could die, get sick or become mentally or physically incapacitated; she could decide to move to Fiji; he could start another business; she could suffer a personal bankruptcy; he could get divorced and lose an interest in the business to his wife; she could find an irresistible offer and want to sell her share to an outsider; he could decide he just can't work with the other owners.

If owners don't work out these terms beforehand, they could find themselves in for a lengthy and costly court battle that could bring the company to its knees.

In most buy-sell agreements, the remaining partners have the right to purchase the outgoing partner's share, based on a formula you agree on.

Insurance

Fires, floods, earthquakes, hurricanes, tornadoes and theft happen, but they always victimize someone else on CNN, right?

Don't bet on it.

Don't let a disaster kill your business. When it comes to insurance as part of your firm foundation:

• Find out everything that's available for your business; and

• Assume nothing about your current coverage.

If you work at home, have a detailed conversation with your insurance agent to find out exactly how much of your business equipment your homeowner's policy covers. As you'll discover, it probably won't cover much–perhaps up to $2,500 of business equipment, and no coverage for business liability. You might be able to add an endorsement to your homeowner's coverage to increase coverage of business equipment but, at some point, you'll need a separate policy for your business.

Whenever you buy a computer or other equipment for your home business, call your agent to make sure it's covered. Evaluate your insurance coverage at least every six months to a year. In some states, you now can buy an in-home business insurance policy that includes liability coverage. Also, if you use your car for business, check with your agent to make sure you're covered there.

For both in-home and out-of-home businesses, spend time networking with colleagues to find out what insurance they have and what else is available. Colleagues might offer tips for how you can save money, as well as recommend a knowledgeable, helpful agent. An association in your field might sponsor insurance programs geared toward your business' needs.

One type of insurance people drop the ball on—both for their personal and business needs—is flood insurance. Most people assume they're covered under their property insurance policies, and that's usually wrong.

Of course, now you're going to make sure you have all your property covered. But did you know you also can buy business interruption insurance that will compensate you for lost income after a disaster? It compensates you for the profits you would have earned if the disaster had not struck.

You'll need to make decisions about what insurance you wish to pay for and what you're willing to risk. However, as part of your business plan, plan what you will do in case of disasters.

A drawing your child makes is worthless to someone else, yet priceless to you. Likewise, your business records have little monetary value, but mean the world to your business. Don't let a disaster rip them away from you. Keep copies of vital papers, as well as all computerized records, in a secure place off site. Update your backup copies frequently.

Better Late Than Never

If you are already in business and did not establish the proper form of legal ownership and put contracts in place, it's not too late. Remember, your company might start with one legal form and then need to change as it grows.

It's your responsibility to choose a strong and proper legal foundation. It does make a difference. Your situation is unique, so don't buy shoes that fit your neighbor but hurt your feet. If your shoes don't fit, a pebble can cripple you. If they do fit, you can step on that pebble and climb the face of a mountain!

Exercise

The legal form of your business organization depends on many factors. Whether you have an existing business or are starting a new business, take this quiz, then head for a business attorney to check on the health of your business' foundation. It might be time to make a change. These questions will not give you an instant answer as to which form of organization you should use, but it will start you in the right direction. Each business is unique, and you need to spend time analyzing your situation with your attorney and CPA.

Business Risk Factors

1. Does your business involve the use of hazardous products (such as pesticides, radioactive wastes, paint, oil, chemicals)?

2. Is your business in an industry that is prone to getting sued often (such as restaurants, bars, medical businesses, doctors' and pharmaceutical companies, real estate agents)?

3. How many employees do you have?

4. Does your business involve unusual risks to your employees (highway workers, construction workers, heavy equipment operators)?

5. List any other risk factors specific to your business.

Decisions

1. Is it important to have total control over your business decisions?

2. Do you feel comfortable sharing the decision-making and profits with other owners?

3. Do you work better alone or with a management team?

4. Are you planning to expand your business by adding more staff or other locations?

Financing

1. Do you have enough personal assets to sustain your business, or do you have sufficient borrowing power to borrow all you need?

2. Will you need money for future expansion?

3. If your business fails, will that put you in personal bankruptcy?

4. Have you explored ways to protect your personal assets from business risks?

Continuity

1. If you are unable to work for any reason, do you have someone reliable who could take your place either temporarily or permanently?

2. Do you expect your business to support you when you retire from actively participating in the day-to-day management?

3. Do you want your family members to continue with your business when you die, and do they want to?

4. Would you like to be able to sell part of your business to raise capital?

The Ninth Commandment

"Where no counsel is, the people fall; but in the multitude of counselors there is safety."
— Proverbs, *Holy Bible*

"Counsel woven into the fabric of real life is wisdom."
— Walter Benjamin, *The Storyteller*

The day was finally near. Harry excitedly told me of the upcoming opening of his new men's clothing store. As I listened to his plans, the idea sounded great. Then, he said ...

"I'm saving a lot of money because my Aunt Mabel is going to do all my bookkeeping at her house!"

"Is Aunt Mabel a CPA?"

"No," he answered.

"Does she have bookkeeping experience?"

"No, but she was good in math in high school, and she has the time."

I told him he should reconsider this idea, but he didn't.

Six months later, Harry rushed into my office.

"Marguerite!" he said in a panic. "The IRS showed up at my store. Said they were going to close me down because I had not paid employee taxes. I'm scared! I paid all my employees. I just didn't know I had to make tax deposits each month! They say I owe $27,000, plus penalties of $12,000. Oh, and the state comptroller called–said something about sales tax deposits. Help!"

Harry suffers from what I now call "Aunt Mabel Syndrome," or AMS for short. This condition strikes when you hire someone in a key position who will work for peanuts, which saves wages or professional fees but almost inevitably costs you a bundle in the long run because of a lack of knowledge and lack of experience.

AMS strikes entrepreneurs repeatedly. Usually, when affected business owners call me, the company is so deep in tax debt that the protection of bankruptcy court is the only option.

This should never happen, but I see it every week in my office. There's a fine line between being frugal and being cheap, and crossing it could end up costing you your business.

So, which professional advisers do you need? These three are essential:

1. Accountant
2. Banker
3. Attorney

How do you choose professional advisers? How do you know who is competent and honest, and charges fair fees? Recommendations from colleagues and friends in business will help. Make sure you interview potential advisers before you hire them, and interview at least three in each area to have a basis for comparison.

In selecting any adviser, use the following as a checklist:

1. Credentials. Check their certifications and backgrounds. What schools did they attend? What degrees or designations do they have? Degrees alone are not enough, but, if you interview someone with no degrees or who won't discuss her educational background, leave!

2. Fees. Fees should be explained clearly, and price structures should be specific. Attorneys and accountants should give you a range of costs for the services you desire. Do not agree to an hourly rate with no ceiling unless you possess unlimited wealth and do not mind parting with it. Ask if you are charged by the job or by the hour. What will you be billed for, and at what rate? Of course, get it in writing.

3. Experience. Ask what experience they have in your area of business. Ask for a list of customer referrals, and call them. Experience in your type of business is invaluable. Beware of advisers who do "everything." Often, they do nothing well.

4. Competence. Experience in small-business issues is essential, but successful experience is even more vital. Do you want an accountant who has prepared books for 300 businesses, and 200 of those have been audited?

5. Communication. You should understand each move your adviser makes, and be informed of developments that affect your business. If an adviser tries to impress you with technical language you don't understand, find another. You are paying for a service–not to be impressed with words. The use of technical jargon suggests the person lacks personal communication and human relations skills. It's your business, and it's essential to understand what advisers are doing for you. If you don't understand, it's your responsibility to ask for clarification.

6. Caring. Be sure advisers show a personal interest in your business as well as in you. You are depending on this person for technical and emotional support. You will be asking advice at turning points in your business and in your life. You must feel your adviser genuinely cares about you, not just your money.

7. Availability. Do they have time for your business? Will they give you prompt service and return your calls? Are they available when you need them? Often, business decisions cannot wait for convenient times.

For example, Robert called his attorney, Sam, at 3 on Friday afternoon because the IRS levied on his business account. Robert needed to pay his employees Saturday. Sam was out of the office, but his staff found him and told him of

Robert's emergency. Sam immediately returned Robert's call and was able to give his client the advice he needed.

Once you decide which advisers to use, to reduce costs, go prepared to talk to them. Be aware of how to use them for your special purposes. Ask specific questions in their areas of expertise.

Here are some suggestions for how to use specific professionals:

Accountants

First, be sure your accountant is qualified–you don't want a bookkeeper for tax advice. Then, bite the bullet and spend the extra money on a CPA with adequate experience in your field. It will save you money in the long haul.

Your accountant can give you advice on:

1. The tax implications of the legal form of your business.

2. Small-business start-up procedure, such as tax registrations with U.S., state and local agencies for income tax, sales tax, franchise tax and property tax.

3. Projecting income and expenses, including a profit and loss statement, and cash-flow projections.

4. Tax planning, including ways to save taxes and stay up to date on tax law changes that could affect you.

5. How to set up your office bookkeeping system. (She might recommend a bookkeeper.)

6. Ways to increase profitability.

7. How to solve problems.

8. How to prepare your tax returns (or she will prepare them for you).

Use your accountant wisely. You are paying her for her experience and education. Do not use her for routine chores that could be handled in a less expensive way. For example, many small businesses can use payroll services for writing checks and handling quarterly tax reporting requirements.

Check out the payroll service as you would a professional adviser.

Bankers

Your choice of banker can be critical to the success of your business.

Changes in our credit system have resulted in the breakdown of personalized banking relations. As recently as the 1970s, bank presidents knew their customers. You could always depend on the stability of your banker–if he had changed banks, rumors would have started and we would all have wondered why he moved on.

Prior to 1975, banks made lending decisions based not only on financial statements, but also on reputation, character and future potential. Bankers believed in us and helped us make it.

Today, most banks change names and personnel frequently. Loan officers are often young, inexperienced and fearful of action. They often come from other communities and don't know the reputations of their clientele, nor do they care. They worry about pleasing bank examiners. They worry about pleasing the corporations they work for, which are often located states away. Their authority also has been diminished, as loans are approved at the corporate level. All of this leaves the majority of small-business owners in the cold, having to rely on either Small Business Administration-approved loans, or credit card cash advances.

Although the mergers continue, we are starting to see small, independent banks cropping up again. Despite the presence of the mega-banks, many of these independents are thriving and ready to help small businesses. The best thing you can do is bank at one of these independents, and build a relationship with the president and loan officers. A study by the Federal Reserve and the SBA found that two-thirds of small businesses again are depending on banks for financing.

In an SBA research study on the profitability of small-business lending by small banks, researchers reported these banks (those with total assets of less than $100 million) earn higher profit rates on small-business loans than on other assets, and these loans significantly increased bank profits by providing cash flow.

The SBA Office of Advocacy conducted a study of banks responsive to small businesses and ranked the top small-business-friendly banks by state. While the majority of the list is made up of small, independent banks, several large, national banks are included. The SBA is a good source of information about banks.

Be sure you find a good bank. Check out the bank's financials; you want to make sure the bank is solvent. Visit with the president. If that isn't possible, visit with the highest-ranking bank officer you can reach. Ask other business owners for referrals. After interviewing several banks, pick the one that best suits your needs, open checking accounts there and begin establishing a relationship. A strong relationship with your banker will assure you better access to credit.

How do you establish and maintain a good relationship with your banker? First and foremost, by opening a healthy line of communication. Communicate with your banker when times are good, and when times are hard. The banker needs to feel secure in your relationship. Invite your banker to your business. Give her a tour of your facilities, and be sure she understands what you do. If your business regularly experiences seasonal ups and downs, make sure she knows that. Then, if you need to extend the due date on a loan or skip a payment during a slow season, she will know why and might help you.

Keep your banker informed. Furnish him copies of your profit and loss statements and tax returns before he asks for them. Keep him up to date on accounts receivable. Let him know the status of all assets pledged to the loan. Show him how heavily you are involved in your business, and that you keep good financial records. Remember, in any relationship, trust is the foundation. If your banker trusts you, he is more likely to help you when you need it.

One of my small-business clients was slipping over the edge toward bankruptcy when his banker volunteered to pull him out. The banker had worked with my client since he started his business in a garage. Rapid changes in the market caused my client financial distress. His banker believed he could make it and, together, they did it. Today, the company is thriving because of the bond my client built with his banker. Remember this checklist:

1. Pick a small, solvent, independent bank that caters to small businesses.

2. Develop a relationship with your banker.

3. Meet the other loan officers so you will know them if your banker leaves.

4. Keep your banker informed, and be sure she understands your business cycle. Let your banker know when times are good, such as when you land a new account. Don't call her just when you are in trouble.

5. Give your banker a balanced picture of your business.

6. Establish a line of credit when you don't need it so you will have it when you do.

7. Always go into the bank looking professional and successful.

Attorneys

Choosing an attorney can be confusing, especially with the deluge of advertising. The best way is to get a referral from someone you trust. Try to avoid calling the local bar-referral service, which is nothing more than an advertising vehicle for lawyers. Avoid lawyers who are in court all the time and do not promptly return your calls. And, don't hire an attorney because he is a friend, or is a friend of the family. Here are questions you should ask:

1. Does she have ample experience and expertise in business law, or specialize in the area you need?
2. Is she board certified in your area of need?
3. Is she well respected by her peers?
4. Is she well respected by court personnel?
5. Did a phone call to the attorney's office leave you feeling that the attorney and staff care, and are competent and experienced?
6. At the initial visit, did the attorney completely and patiently answer all questions and give you adequate information, time and attention, or did you detect an emotional distance? Remember: there are no stupid questions, so be sure all questions were asked and answered.
7. Do you feel comfortable with your attorney?
8. Was the fee structure explained completely, and are you comfortable with the fees? Was an estimate of costs given to you?
9. Do you feel confident the attorney will work in your best interest?

Special Situations, Special Attorneys

A general business attorney cannot cover all needs. Most businesses need attorneys with specialized knowledge. Here are three examples:

Immigration Attorney

LoLis Vargas, of the Flying Vargas Family, needs an immigration attorney. As the family travels all year in circuses throughout the world, their children are born in different countries. It's difficult enough with one visa or passport, so imagine crossing a border with an array. To work in each place, they all need work permits. LoLis, manager of the business, knows a good, qualified immigration attorney in each country her family visits.

Intellectual Property

If your business involves the written word, anything artistic or the creation of ideas, you need to develop a relationship with an intellectual property attorney. In the areas of copyright, trademark and patents, laws vary from country to country, so don't assume anything.

Business Reorganization

The hardest time to seek legal help usually is when a business is facing financial problems. If you have financial struggles, seek the help of an attorney who specializes in business reorganization. If you get the right advice early enough, you might solve your problems. If your business is in financial trouble, or might be headed that way, consult the Financial First Aid Kit at the back of this book and learn how to best use your attorney's expertise to help you.

Other Advisers

If you are running a small business, especially a one- or two-person shop, you also need to realize you can't do everything yourself. There are only so many hours in the day, you need vacations, and unexpected situations such as illnesses are guaranteed to happen.

One of the reasons people become entrepreneurs is to have more control over their financial lives, but they often take that philosophy too far–"I'll do it all myself." Not only can't you do it all, it's often a bad move financially. Business owners should focus their attention on the most profitable parts of the business and turn over the rest of the details to others. Business owners need to admit two things: they shouldn't handle tasks others can take care of at a cheaper hourly rate, and employees or contractors are simply better at some parts of the business than they are!

From the start, build relationships with other professionals who can handle the parts of the business you don't have the time, expertise or equipment for. You'll turn to some of these people every day as employees. You'll turn to others, such as contractors and vendors, as needed. But they all need to be part of your team.

Other teammates might include public relations agents, insurance agents, printers, computer specialists, marketing professionals, package shipping companies, long-distance telephone service and Internet service providers, and mailing houses.

You also might want to appoint an advisory board to help guide your business. Perhaps you could gather a financial adviser, attorney, banker or several trusted colleagues a few times a year to review where your business stands now, and where it is headed.

The cost of hiring professionals is an investment in your business. You are building a professional team, a support system that should pay off in a healthier, more prosperous business. You are choosing professionals you trust to help you solve problems, and to guide you through important decisions.

You will be spending a great deal of time working with these professionals and their staffs–choose wisely!

Stop Aunt Mabel Syndrome before it stops you. Your generous contribution to your business is appreciated. Thank you.

Exercise

Do you have all the professional advisers you need in place, particularly your accountant, banker and attorney? If not, begin asking colleagues for referrals and set up interviews. Write a list of other advisers you need to begin developing a relationship with–do it now, long before you need them. What parts of the business are you spending time on now that you could turn over to an employee or independent contractor to free your time for more profitable pursuits?

The Tenth Commandment

Learn to Turn Coal Into Gold

"All risings to a great place are by a winding stair."
—Francis Bacon, *Essays of Great Place*

"I don't like people who have never fallen or stumbled. Their virtue is lifeless and isn't of much value. Life hasn't revealed its beauty to them."
—Boris Pasternak, *Doctor Zhivago*

Life gives us a lot to work with. We build and mold our lives with our emotions, our experiences, our beliefs. Picture three different children, each with a ball of Play-Doh. One throws it against the wall. Another squishes it into something shapeless in her hands, then squishes it more. One plays with it awhile, places it aside, thinks about it, then goes back and shapes it into a castle.

Each of us has a ball of Play-Doh. We choose to build castles or do nothing. Some who choose to do nothing make excuses, such as, "I can't succeed, but he did because he has more education." Or, "She's better looking." Or, "Her parents had money. We were poor."

Everyone has advantages and disadvantages. Failures and losses happen to everyone. So, what makes the difference?

It's all in how we view our experiences.

Conquering Mountains, Conquering Challenges
Ron had a successful home-building company. An active and athletic man, he supervised each custom home, watching all parts of the building process carefully. One summer, he took two months off to fulfill a dream of climbing Mount Everest. Before he reached the top, he suffered a fall that left him paralyzed from the waist down.

Did Ron's business suffer because of his loss of mobility? No, because Ron decided not to let that happen. In fact, Ron developed a new mission in life. Today, his company builds beautiful custom homes for people with physical disabilities. His clients are thrilled to have someone who understands their needs build their homes.

It's important to learn from events, both good and bad, in our lives. The experience in and of itself means nothing, but your perception of the experience makes all the difference in the world.

Remember Mr. Roper, the 70-year-old inventor we met in Chapter Two who builds mosquito houses? Here's a man who literally takes all of life's junk and turns it into something useful. As with the intent of the new machine he's working on, Roper is able to convert coal into gold, all because he is able to look at waste in a way that benefits himself and others.

Turning coal into gold means we savor the lesson, but dump the emotional garbage that goes with it. Your money, your business, all of life goes in cycles. It is important to accept that you will have ups and downs. It is inevitable. Learn to see your business cycles from a great distance, as if looking down from a plane. On the highway, all you might see is an endless traffic jam. But, from the air, you can see the clear road just ahead.

Each and every one of us will experience tragedies and failures in life and in business. Depending on how you view them, you might be able to look back someday and admit that many of these were valuable turning points that you wouldn't trade for anything. But that takes time and perspective. When a crisis occurs, we must handle it first before moving on to the next step.

Handling Crises Productively

A crisis is defined as a turning point in the course of anything; a decisive or crucial time; a moment of truth. Note that the definition does not have a negative connotation. A crisis is simply an event that gives you a chance to change your life.

If you are going through a crisis now, you are probably thinking, "Great! I am in the middle of a mess and she is talking about improving my life." So let's get through the crisis first. A small-business owner cannot insulate his business from his personal life. Even a personal crisis will affect an owner's on-the-job performance.

Whether you fall off a ladder outside or find yourself amid a financial mess, the steps to recovery are the same:

1. Notice the symptoms and recognize the injury needs attention.
2. Take the steps necessary to heal.
3. Be patient and allow time to heal.

How Does A Crisis Hit You?

First, there is the physical impact. Your stomach might feel sick. You can't eat, or you overeat. You might be drinking more than usual or taking pills to dull your senses. You have trouble sleeping, or sleep too much. Your head pounds. Your heart races.

Then, there's the emotional side. You feel you can't cope with the situation and don't know where to turn. You might be angry and frustrated with family members, other people or yourself. You might wish to be alone–being with people doesn't help you feel better. You find it hard to concentrate on work. Your energy and emotions might plunge from high to low without warning. A crisis not only creates feelings about the immediate problem, but also stirs old emotions.

Common feelings reported by those going through a business financial crisis are:

out of control	depressed
abused	afraid
distrusting	angry
isolated	lonely
doomed	moody
hurt	persecuted
incompetent	victimized
guilty	unhappy
frustrated	defensive
vulnerable	suspicious
lethargic	overwhelmed
exhausted	disappointed in yourself and others

It is important to be able to express these feelings to someone you trust–be it a counselor, minister, friend, spouse or someone who has been through a similar crisis. You do not want condemnation, which will only intensify your feelings and make you feel more guilty. You simply want someone who will listen.

If you don't have someone you can trust with your feelings, write them down in a journal. It will help. When a crisis hits, I can go back to the last crisis in my journal and read, knowing I got through it. I can read what I learned from the crisis. It gives me a different perspective and lets me know that, "This too shall pass."

Many of the personal and business activities we've discussed earlier in the book will help when a crisis hits. Your greatest ally in tough times will be your values and priorities. If you have the big picture in perspective, chances are better you will be able to handle what life throws at you, and turn it to your benefit.

A crisis is rough on your body, both physically and emotionally. As you work through the crisis and let go of some of the emotional trauma, your body will begin to feel better. In the meantime, do what you can to avoid further physical stress. While the following suggestions are always good for your lifestyle, they are especially vital during times of crisis:

1. Eat well. Take a look at what you are eating. Avoid junk food. Any foods you're sensitive to will affect you more drastically, making it harder for you to cope. Eat small meals you can easily digest. Be sure to include low-fat proteins and many fresh fruits and vegetables. Take a supplement to help you get adequate vitamins B, C, D and others in your diet.

2. Exercise. Don't try to run a marathon if you never exercise. Start slowly, perhaps with walking. When you exercise, your body releases natural chemicals that elevate your mood. Many report lifting weights helps reduce stress and gives them a feeling of control. Exercise also will help you sleep better.

3. Avoid or limit alcohol. Yes, alcohol might make you feel better now, but it's no long-term solution. Studies have shown that alcohol depresses the body the next day. If you drink nightly, you will feel physically and emotionally depressed the next day, and the stress cycle continues. If you choose to drink, do so in moderation and stick to beer or wine.

4. Reduce caffeine intake. Drinking cola, coffee or anything high in caffeine can make you more tense. Caffeine makes it harder to sleep, which then motivates some to drink alcohol or take drugs. Often, people under stress get into a destructive caffeine/alcohol cycle. Try exercise instead of drinking alcohol or caffeine at night. Vigorous exercise followed by a hot bath or shower about 7 p.m. will help you sleep better when 10 p.m. rolls around.

5. Express your emotions. Find a safe haven where no one will disturb you, and cry if you want to. Don't keep your frustrations bottled inside.

6. Rest. Try to get plenty of rest. It is difficult to sleep when you have a lot of questions on your mind. Try writing the questions on a piece of paper and choose to handle them in the morning, not while you're trying to get some shuteye. If you are having trouble falling asleep, get up and do something. Read a book or soak in a hot tub. Don't just lie in bed and worry. Do not take sleeping pills unless both you and your doctor believe they are necessary.

7. Try methods of relaxation and stress reduction. There are many helpful audio tapes on the market that help you relax, step by step. This might be a time to try something new.

Be Patient

Your crisis will not disappear before your eyes. Ron, the home-builder who became paralyzed, took more than a year to rehabilitate his mind and body before heading back to work. Then, and only then, was he able to focus on the future. He went through many emotions, ups and downs, in the healing process.

The process of change involves breaking apart the puzzle and putting it together in new and better ways. We always resist change, especially if it is painful. Acknowledge the pain and move through it, having faith that, when the crisis is over, you will be wiser and have a new beginning in life.

It's your choice. You can see a crisis as a devastating experience and learn nothing from it (people who choose this will repeat the same mistakes), or you can choose to see any crisis as a positive learning experience that makes you stronger, and gives you freedom from old beliefs and habits that were not working for you. Lewis Carroll, in *Alice's Adventures in Wonderland*, wrote, "Everything has got a moral, if you can only find it."

New Beginnings

In the book *Resilience,* Dr. Frederic Falch, M.D., reported that, in working with patients, he began to see falling apart and depression as a necessary step of personal renewal after stressful events. Through counseling with his patients, Falch saw that our life is a cycle of coming apart and putting the pieces back together in new form. A new picture can be created, but life needs to fall apart before it can be rebuilt.

Many patients collapsed in the face of stress and appeared thoroughly defeated. Falch found out, however, that this was a necessary step in healing old wounds–these tragedies were often the result of old behavioral patterns and past programming sabotaging their lives. In exploring these issues, the patients discovered new and better ways to deal with life.

Falch stated that all stressful times are, by their nature, disruptive. Disruption is built into the process, because we have strong forces pulling on us: One force wants to keep things exactly as they are, while the other calls us to move forward and let go of the past. When we go through psychological stress, those changes lead to a stronger mental structure. We can learn something from what we have been through and emerge reorganized and stronger.

Many successful business owners experienced financial crises before they became successful–and many others will fail and rebuild again. The crisis called attention to the problem so they could learn, make adjustments and turn the coal into gold.

"Coal to gold" is a simple metaphor for transforming something that seems dark and devoid of life into something bright and valuable. Just as coal has the potential to warm us by fire, so life's dark experiences can transform us into better people. We then become like the mythical bird, the Phoenix, reborn out of the fire of life's events.

Every day, we make choices on how we interpret events in our lives. As Henry David Thoreau said, "Things do not change; we change."

In my years of law practice and counseling people in trouble, I have seen a common denominator among those who survive crises in a healthy manner: They use the challenges to create gold.

Consider the following examples:

After 15 years of a successful career, with four wonderful teenage children and a happy marriage, John had to file bankruptcy for his company. He lost his job and every cent of retirement money. After handling the emotional loss, John and his family turned the coal into gold. They moved to a lake and opened a bait store, giving John more time with his family, and dreams and goals they could all share. This new business is thriving because John learned his lessons and loves what he is doing. A new life arose from the rubble.

Sandra's divorce was difficult. She and her two pre-teenage children spent much time in therapy, sorting life out. Instead of dwelling on the feelings of misery, guilt and loss, Sandra focused on what they learned about communication and the strength of pulling together. She and the children acquired many communication skills and developed a stronger family bond. Recognizing the value of communication, Sandra returned to school and obtained a Ph.D. in psychology. Today, she owns a successful business, a family counseling practice.

While we have focused on the extremes, the coal-to-gold example can be used in everyday occurrences. It brought a grin to my face recently when my 19-year-old son saw the bright side of an annoying experience. When his car transmission collapsed, he called from college and said, "Mom, the bad news is my car fell apart and is in the shop, but don't worry, I am getting it taken care of. The good news is, out of necessity, I have learned Texas A & M has a great bus system. It can get me where I need to go. Now, I'm not dependent on my car."

Remember coal-to-gold to reduce stress in either drastic or everyday situations:

Coal	Gold
Losing your job.	A chance to change careers and start that business you've dreamed of.
Stuck in traffic.	A time to listen to that tape on how to improve sales.
An irate customer makes a scene in your store.	A chance for you to handle a problem while employees are watching so next time they can do it properly.
Hitting rock-bottom.	Great! The only way to go is up.

To turn "Coal to Gold" in a stressful situation:

1. Stop. Pause and take a deep breath.
2. Listen to any messages from your body and your intuition.
3. Act to take care of immediate needs.
4. Step back and see if you have done the best you can.
5. Turn the Coal into Gold. Expect something positive and embrace the crisis as an opportunity and challenge to find the gold.

Is this living in a fantasy world? Are we ignoring reality? No! You are taking care of the crisis in the best possible way, but you decide not to roll around in the garbage. Instead, you choose to plant seeds and expect the flowers to grow out of the manure. It is a way to allow yourself to be open to learning from a situation. It is much healthier and causes less stress on your body.

Even death can be gold of the finest quality. I sat with my father, holding his hand, when he died at home. In two days, we healed a lifetime of hurt. As I watched him die and leave his body, my soul traveled part way with him before I felt the need to return. I will never forget that wonderful experience. It changed my life.

Exercise

List 10 instances of events you would call "coal" in your life, then go back and list the "gold" you found in each when looking at the situation years later.

Bonus Chapter

Your Financial First-Aid Kit: What to Do if Major Financial Trouble Strikes

Business owners like to think about success. They do not like to dwell on potential financial problems. Yet, most small businesses will face financial crises. Some businesses will survive, some won't.

This bonus chapter explains your options when a financial crisis hits. It you're headed for financial trouble or are already there, know your options and seek qualified help immediately! Your quick action might save your business.

If your business can't pay its bills, and you are out of available cash and credit, these are your options.

Let's look at an example:

Don and Betty have a store called, "The Magic Tree" in a mall. They sell children's stuffed animals and had been successful for many years. On Jan. 15, they realized that the all-important December holiday sales were down drastically from past years, and they did not make enough money to carry them through the annual lag in sales during the first quarter of the new year. They barely covered December expenses and know they lack income to pay bills for January, February and March. By Feb. 1, they had fallen behind in their bills and creditors were calling, several of them threatening to sue. What can they do?

Let's look at their options:

1. Pay no one and ignore creditors

Can they continue business as usual? If Don and Betty fail to pay the rent, the mall landlord will lock up the store. If they fail to pay suppliers and distributors, they won't receive more teddy bears, so they won't have anything to sell. If they fail to pay their loans on inventory, the creditor will repossess the inventory. If they fail to pay utility bills, they will find their store in the dark.

Ignoring financial problems will not work. If they don't take action now, it will be too late for their enterprise.

2. Disappear

Close the doors, disappear and do not pay anybody. Amazingly, some people try this option. They might leave town, or take off for Mexico or some Caribbean island.

Even though the store creditors might not be able to sue them personally because the business was incorporated, Don and Betty and "The Magic Tree" are now out of business. The question is: how will Don and Betty survive? What type of income will they have?

The landlord and other creditors will file lawsuits against the store, and against Don and Betty if they have personally guaranteed anything. A creditor might wrongfully sue them personally and, if they don't answer the lawsuit, the creditor can get a personal judgment against them. So, their personal credit and the store credit will be ruined.

Running away is a dangerous option that creates problems that will plague you for the rest of your life. While we all might want to run away at one time or another, this should never be an option.

3. Put out immediate fires

Pay only the "squeaky wheels." If the creditor who distributes teddy bears is calling, pay him, but don't pay the creditors who are not bothering them yet. Pay the landlord because she can lock up the store. Pay the utilities.

Will this work? Maybe for a while (and it's absolutely a better choice than the previous two). This might buy some time for Don and Betty while they are deciding what to do. However, if they try to do a workout with their creditors later, or file for bankruptcy, this approach would create problems that would be hard to overcome. The biggest drawback is that it would send a bad-faith message to creditors and impede other options.

4. Secure a debt consolidation loan

This might work, but the high costs of such a loan, as well as the risks, should be carefully analyzed with your CPA and attorney before making this move. Otherwise, you might be doing nothing more than postponing an inevitable business failure. Debt consolidation loans also can be difficult for a business to obtain if problems are too far along. As with regular loans, they're easier to obtain when you don't need them.

5. Create a creditor workout

There are many advantages to a workout if the funds exist, but some of the requirements for success are beyond your control.

First, all creditors must agree to the workout. If this happens, Don and Betty can continue with their business as long as they make scheduled payments under the workout plan.

Second, workout plans should follow the same form as a bankruptcy reorganization plan so that later, if Don and Betty must file for bankruptcy reorganization, they can follow the same plan.

To determine if a workout is feasible, you must analyze your financial problems:

1. Immediate threats. Are taxes due, or is the IRS threatening to levy?

2. Endurance. Will your business generate enough money to allow you to survive your workout and move on?

3. Economy. What do economic conditions say about your chances of surviving a workout?

4. Timing. Does your business cycle leave the probability that your cash flow will increase enough to pay creditors and let you move on to business as usual?

How to Develop a Workout Plan

- Determine sources of money available.
- Examine cash flow.
- Spell out alternative plans if workout fails.
- Determine what financials to disclose to creditors.
- List creditors and what amount is owed.
- List assets with current value.
- Update your business plan.
- Spell out what reorganization will be done.
- Show what creditors will get in a Chapter 7 bankruptcy to convince them a workout is more advantageous for them.
- Show sources of cash for workout payments.
- Finally, negotiate with creditors, get them to sign releases and implement the plan.

Need for Professional Help

If you plan a workout agreement, use professionals for these reasons:

Accountants
- Your accountant will keep records of payments required by your plan.

Attorneys
- An attorney lends validity to your plan.
- An attorney will take steps to ensure workout agreements are binding.

• An attorney can make sure your workout will not prejudice your right to file for bankruptcy if necessary.

Types of Workouts

There are many ways to structure out-of-court workouts. The following are common:

1. Liquidation. Assets no longer essential for operation of the newly restructured business are sold, and creditors look to these for financial recovery.
2. Creditors take ownership in the company. In some cases, creditors can be given ownership rights in place of your debt. Debtors often propose stock in exchange for debt elimination. For small businesses, this usually won't work, as creditors probably won't want stock in a struggling business.
3. Collateral can be transferred to secured creditors for full satisfaction of the debt. Before agreeing to this, the secured creditors will want to look at your cash flow to be sure this puts them in a better position than waiting for a longer payout.
4. Lump-sum payback. Creditors might agree to accept a lesser amount if paid in a lump sum. The debtor will take cash assets and prorate them among creditors. Creditors usually will accept a smaller amount under this plan than they would under a long-term payout because they will get money sooner. This plan can help the debtor become debt-free quicker.
5. Short-term monthly payments. Creditors are given payments over a short period of time. The total percentage they are to receive depends on the value of the business and the amount of profit it expects to make in the future. Creditors are asked to postpone debt collection as well as state-court rights to give the debtor the chance to continue business. This puts creditors in the position of investing in the debtor's future.

6. Long-term repayment. Creditors might be agreeable to taking a note for repayment of your debt plus interest over a longer period of time. Trade creditors might require that a debtor pay back a certain percentage on the old debt, as well as make the debtor pay cash for new supplies.

7. Internal Revenue Service restructuring. If the debtor owes back taxes, an agreement with the IRS must be made before proposing a workout to other creditors. Creditors will want assurance the IRS won't close down the business.

Internal Sources of Money for a Workout

• Reduce costs. Eliminate unnecessary employees, shop around for supplies to obtain the most favorable prices, and trim unnecessary costs.

• Collect receivables. If necessary, bargain with companies whose receivables seem to be uncollectable. At this point, it is better to collect something than nothing at all. Keep billing current–delinquent billing often results in late payments.

• Sell equipment. For example, sell vehicles that are not being used or out-of-date equipment that another company might buy.

• Liquidate inventory. Even though you might take a loss, you will be moving the inventory and pumping new money back into the business.

• Reduce salaries of officers and directors.

External Sources of Money for a Workout

• Trade creditors and suppliers. If your problem lies with short-term cash flow, consult with your trade creditors and ask for more time to pay your bills. When you ask for additional time, be prepared to pay cash for future shipments.

• Bank credit. Very difficult to obtain when you are in financial trouble.

• Investors. This is risky unless you know the investors well, because they will want to participate in management of the business.

• Owners' and stockholders' funds. This can be a temporary source of capital, but it can cause long-term problems if personal bills are ignored.

Advantages of a Workout

1. Faster and cheaper than using the bankruptcy court.
2. Flexible.
3. Professional fees usually less than in bankruptcy proceedings.
4. Shows good faith to creditors.
5. No formal court proceedings or government supervision.
6. Usually does not affect a business' value.
7. Debtor retains control of the business.

Disadvantages of a Workout

1. Debtor has to get 100 percent creditor consent.
2. Debtor is not protected by bankruptcy court from lawsuits or other actions during the workout period.
3. Debtor might need a new source of funds to make the plan succeed.
4. If a debtor can't stick to the plan, major trouble is ahead. The possibility of receiving payment has made creditors cooperate, but if the debtor is unable to live up to the promises, creditors might take fast action to collect.

I am often asked, "Will the threat of bankruptcy force creditors into a workout?" Ten or 15 years ago, this was a real threat to creditors, but it doesn't work much anymore. Often, in Texas, if I call a creditor and tell him we are considering bankruptcy but would like to sit down and talk, he will say, "Why don't you go ahead and file the bankruptcy, and we'll get our attorney to take care of it." The overwhelming number of bad debts many creditors must deal with often hinders their willingness to consider a workout.

If a workout is not feasible, only three alternatives remain for Don and Betty:

6. Close the Company

Don and Betty can liquidate the company out of court. They can close the doors, sell all their assets and distribute the money to creditors on a prorated basis. Many creditors would rather have something than nothing. However, this plan probably won't work if all creditors can't be paid in full, as it does not prevent lawsuits.

7. Sell the Business

A common misconception is that an owner can sell a business and walk away with clean hands. It often isn't that easy.

If you sell your business, most states require that creditors are notified of the pending sale. Some states require that all creditors must approve of the sale unless they will be paid in full immediately afterward.

So, Don and Betty can't sell "The Magic Tree" to Stewart for $100,000 if they have $150,000 in debt, unless they comply with state law. Stewart could end up being responsible for all company debts. Don and Betty would still be responsible for personal guarantees, taxes and other debts, depending on the legal structure of their business. Don, Betty and Stewart all could be subject to fraud charges if they didn't comply with state law.

If you want to sell your business, you must get legal help or you could end up with no business and a stack of debts.

8. Declare Bankruptcy

The bankruptcy code is divided into chapters, each representing a different type. Each has its own requirements and court process.

Briefly, Chapter 7 is a "straight bankruptcy," or liquidation; Chapter 11 defines the requirements and steps in the process of business reorganization; Chapter 12 is a special type of bankruptcy available for farmers, allowing them protection while they file a plan to reorganize debts and repay creditors; Chapter 13, often referred to as a wage earner or small-business reorganization plan, gives a sole proprietorship or individual time to pay creditors through the court by filing a plan of monthly payments. The amount of debt is limited.

Bankruptcy has its own language. Here are some terms used by every bankruptcy court and lawyer:

Automatic Stay

When a new case is taken to bankruptcy court and presented to the clerk for filing, it is stamped with that day's date. Immediately upon filing, the automatic stay comes into effect. The automatic stay is a law in the bankruptcy code that states the debtor is protected from any action by creditors against his or her property. This action stops the following:

1. Lawsuits. There can be no further proceedings against the debtor in related issues, such as the continuation of a lawsuit, the filing of a complaint, the taking of depositions, or a trial.

2. Judgments or garnishments. This stops the enforcement of judgments obtained before the case was filed, including garnishments of wages or bank accounts.

3. Property repossession. A creditor cannot obtain or enforce property liens against the debtor.

4. Collection action. The stay stops any action to collect, assess or recover claims. This includes harassing creditor

phone calls, as well as indirect pressure such as contacting the debtor's friends, relatives, neighbors or employees.

5. Set-offs. For example, if a debtor owes money to a bank and has money in an account in that bank, the bank may not take the money in his account and "set it off"–apply it against the debt owed–without filing a "Motion to Lift Stay."

6. Tax collection actions. Any tax-court proceedings halt.

There are exceptions to the automatic stay, but they are not listed here because of their complexity. This is just a brief overview of what is covered under the stay.

Motion to Lift Stay

If a creditor wants to foreclose on any of the debtor's property while the debtor is in bankruptcy, the creditor must first go to the bankruptcy court and file a "Motion to Lift Stay." Generally, if the debtor does not answer the motion within 10 days and have a hearing, the stay will be lifted, and the creditor may proceed with foreclosure efforts. To keep the property, the debtor must, among other things, show the court the creditor's secured property is adequately protected and convince the court the creditor should not be allowed to proceed.

Exempt Property

When a bankruptcy is filed, all of the debtor's property becomes property of the bankrupt estate, except property claimed under a schedule of exemptions. Only certain classes of creditors can reach exempt property, such as those who financed the purchase of the property, or certain taxing authorities. The amount of property allowed as exempt differs from state to state.

Only individuals may claim property as exempt, and this usually includes the home and some personal property. Corporations are not allowed exemptions.

Equity in Property

The difference between the market value of property and secured debts against it is called equity. When determining how much property you may exempt, the equity is used, not the market value.

Example:

> Market value of car: $25,000
> Debt against car: $20,000
> Equity: $5,000.

To keep the car, the debtor must have room in his exemptions for the $5,000 equity. In addition, the debtor must continue making car payments during the bankruptcy.

341 Section Creditors Meeting

This is a meeting or hearing in which a trustee, not a judge, presides and questions the debtor about his property and some of his financial problems. Creditors may come and question the debtor. The meeting is named after the section of the bankruptcy code that requires it be held.

Most Common Types of Debt

Secured Debt

This is a debt in which any property is pledged as collateral for its repayment. This can be a voluntary security pledge, such as when you purchase a car, or an involuntary attachment of your property by the IRS for back taxes, or by a creditor who obtains a court judgment then records it in your county property records.

Unsecured Debt

This is a debt for which no property is pledged or held by the creditor. Most credit card debt falls in this category.

Priority Debt

Certain debts in a bankruptcy proceeding are considered priority, meaning this class may be paid before other unsecured debts. Examples of priority debts include taxes and certain recent wages due to employees of the debtor.

Treatment of Secured Property

If a creditor has a security interest in property of an individual debtor (as opposed to a corporate debtor), the debtor might be able to:

1. Void the lien. This can happen on certain personal property if a creditor's security interests were not created at the time of the purchase.

2. Reaffirm the debt. A debtor may reaffirm or re-obligate himself for any debt prior to the discharge in bankruptcy. This means the debt will not be canceled in the bankruptcy and the debtor must continue to pay. A debtor will usually reaffirm the debt on his home, car and appliances. Some debtors wish to reaffirm debts co-signed or guaranteed by friends and/or relatives. Creditors are usually glad to see a debtor reaffirm a debt, but the debtor's attorney or the court must rule it is within the debtor's means to repay.

3. Redeem the property. This can be done by paying the market value of the property, usually in a lump sum, to the secured creditor. A court hearing may be necessary to determine market value, unless the parties agree.

4. Return the property and cancel the debt. The debtor may return the secured property and wipe the debt clear.

Discharge

This is the clean slate and fresh start most debtors are seeking. It means you are no longer legally obligated on the debts listed on your schedules unless you have reaffirmed the debt, or the debts are not discharged by law, or the debts are found non-dischargeable by the court.

Non-dischargeable Debt

This debt is not cancelled by the bankruptcy. It might include taxes, alimony, and certain government guaranteed and funded school loans. A creditor may object to the discharge of certain debts, such as those incurred by fraudulent means. In such a case, the court will have a trial on the issues.

Most Common Types of Bankruptcy

Chapter 7

This is available to most businesses regardless of the amount of debt owed, and is normally used when an individual or corporation has exhausted all resources and is closing the business' doors.

If Don and Betty's business is incorporated, the assets are liquidated by the bankruptcy trustee and the proceeds are divided among creditors in the order set by the bankruptcy code. If Don and Betty run a sole proprietorship, they might be able to keep some property, due to their ability to claim certain property as exempt. A Chapter 7 gives an orderly liquidation of the bankrupt estate by returning collateral to the secured creditors, or liquidating assets and distributing the cash among creditors.

Chapter 11

This is often referred to as a "debtor's reorganization." This option is available to large and small businesses, no matter what the legal organization. Briefly, here are the factors involved in a Chapter 11 filing:

1. The debtor remains in possession of and operation of the business, subject to certain requirements and restrictions by the court;

2. The debtor files monthly reports with the U.S. Trustee's office;

3. The debtor proposes a plan to pay back creditors;

4. This plan is voted on by creditors;

5. The court approves the plan;

6. The debtor begins to pay creditors according to the plan.

Chapter 13

Chapter 13 is available to both small businesses and individuals. It is not available to corporations, but it can be used by any small-businessperson whose secured debts do not exceed $750,000 and whose unsecured debts do not exceed $250,000.

In Chapter 13, the business may remain open. The debtor will continue to operate the business and will retain ownership of both exempt and non-exempt property. The owner files a plan with the court that shows the business' operating budget, the owners' personal budget, and details of how much will be paid to each classification of creditor. The main requirement is that the plan must demonstrate the business' best efforts to repay creditors. Chapter 13 offers many advantages over Chapter 11 and is often a good choice for a small, unincorporated business.

Creditors and Bankruptcy

Dealing with creditors is an unavoidable part of every bankruptcy. Therefore, it is important to understand the process from the creditor's point of view.

Creditors are not the enemy unless you make them so. Creditors simply want to get paid. You can work together and create a win-win situation that will help you during, and even after, bankruptcy.

Consulting an Attorney

The best time to seek professional advice is well before you are knee-deep in financial trouble. Whether you have simply spotted warning signs of financial trouble, or you find yourself needing to take drastic measures, it is vital you consult a qualified attorney for direction. Don't try to go it alone.

Most business owners facing financial problems are upset when they consult an attorney. This is a natural reaction to a stressful situation. Clients might feel intimidated and embarrassed, and, as a result, often don't ask the questions they need to ask.

I will give you tips so you can know how to talk to your attorney and get the information you need.

Pick a competent attorney who is well-respected and board certified in the field of business reorganization. You must do your homework first and prepare the detailed financial information your attorney will need to assist you. You need specific answers and specific solutions. Just as a doctor needs to know your symptoms to make a competent diagnosis, an attorney needs financial information to evaluate your situation and recommend a course of action.

What to Take to an Initial Interview

Financial problems cause stress. Stress can cause you to feel disorganized. To get organized, gather the following information and take it with you when you go to your attorney's office.

1. A complete list of business debts;
2. A list of business assets at present market value. These can be listed by category such as real estate, business equipment, accounts receivable, etc. List your opinion of each asset's market value based on liquidation value. If you have a question as to value, ask a dealer or auctioneer;
3. A list of personal debts and assets for you and your spouse. This is necessary only if your business is not incorporated or if you have personally guaranteed any of your business debts;
4. Copies of any current property leases;
5. Copies of financial statements you have furnished to creditors;

6. A cash-flow statement showing business income and expenses;

7. Copies of legal documents such as notes and security agreements;

8. Lawsuits. Copies of any outstanding actions;

9. Judgments. Paperwork concerning any judgments taken against your company;

10. Taxes. Bring copies of tax bills, including liens sent by the IRS or other taxing authorities. It is also essential to have a copy of the computer printout the IRS keeps on your business account. It reflects everything, including assessment dates, payments, liens and current balances. You can get this from your local tax collection office. Also bring a copy of the previous year's tax return.

Initial Interview

You are in a crisis, financial and emotional, and you need to feel comfortable and confident with your attorney. At the initial visit, the attorney should review the information you have furnished, evaluate your situation and advise you accordingly.

This initial interview should be done by the attorney, not a secretary or legal assistant.

An attorney should not push you into any solution, but should let you know what options are available.

Only you can make the decision. If you feel you are being pushed to file bankruptcy, get a second opinion. The exception would be if you are in the "Red Zone" we discussed in Chapter Five and you have no time left to protect yourself. An example would be a foreclosure or IRS levy within a day or two.

You will want to know what the attorney's services cost. If you don't know the attorney's reputation, ask what experience and education she has had in handling cases similar to yours. Be candid and open. You are trying to find someone you feel comfortable enough with to handle your business and personal financial situation.

What an Attorney Should Do on Your First Visit

1. Give you a chance to explain your problem. Be sure the attorney is a good listener and cares about you;

2. Ask for specific information about your debts and assets;

3. Explain the differences in the types of debts you have;

4. Discuss financial options, including workouts and bankruptcy, and explain the advantages and disadvantages of all options;

5. Explain your chances of success if you wish to do a workout or to reorganize through bankruptcy;

6. Give a brief summary of how you can protect property from creditor attachment in and out of bankruptcy court;

7. Evaluate your business' cash flow;

8. Explain how to value your assets;

9. Explain options for handling your secured assets if you are considering a workout or Chapter 7 bankruptcy;

10. Explain the impact a workout or bankruptcy might have on any cosigners or guarantors.

11. Help you prioritize which bills to pay if you have a cash flow problem;

12. Explain the attorney's fee structure and costs;

13. Give you a chance to ask questions. You MUST be able to ask any questions you have, and get answers you understand.

Personal Experiences in Choosing a Lawyer

The following people needed an attorney to help them in financial crises. Let's look at what they consider important in choosing a lawyer:

One business owner who faced trouble: "When I came to the first visit in the attorney's office, I knew that my company was overwhelmed in debt, and expected to be looked upon as a failure. I was not treated that way at all. Everyone in my attorney's office was friendly, courteous, helpful, understanding and always ready to answer the many questions I had. I knew that they had heard these questions hundreds of times each day. But I felt completely confident that they were doing their best for me in regard to my individual case. Knowing that I was going to be met with a friendly face at the office and at the creditors meeting helped me a great deal. When I called my attorney, they knew who I was. I wasn't treated as just a number. As a result, I felt secure and never doubted my attorney or the staff's expertise. My attorney was available for emergencies when I needed her."

Burt, 54, who succeeded in a workout with creditors: "I advise anyone considering filing to get an attorney who specializes in workouts and bankruptcy. This way, there are no surprises. Choose a well-known attorney, talk to him, and have him guide you in this decision. In a case such as ours, it made all the difference in the world."

Another entrepreneur who had experienced financial problems and successfully reorganized: "There would be a lot of businesses still in operation today if they knew about bankruptcy laws and how they help the debtor and the creditor. It is of no benefit to anyone when a company or an individual just walks away from his debt. I can really thank my attorney, and the staff, for guiding me through so that I could feel successful in the end. We repaid everyone, thanks to my attorney's expertise and emotional support."

Afterword

There really are no new secrets to life. The truth has always been there—it's just stated in new ways. I hope that I've helped some of these secrets get through to you. We can be so obsessed with living the perfect life and having the perfect business that we forget how to live. By following the *10 Commandments of Small-Business Success,* you can enjoy life and have a successful business. While you're working hard and smart, don't forget about the little joys of life.

Remember the 10 Commandments:

Specialize in What You Know and Love
Understand the Entrepreneurial Mindset
Cause Cash to Flow: Create a Sound Business Plan
Comply With Tax Laws—Render Unto Caesar!
Expect the Unexpected: Learn to Recognize Problems
Seize Prosperity: Learn How to Create Money
Seek Silence in Chaos
Form a Firm Foundation
Use Professional Advisers
Learn to Turn Coal Into Gold

These 10 Commandments will help you overcome obstacles and avoid problems before they happen. Remember to write them down and review them each day. If you'd like a free "10 Commandments" certificate, suitable for framing for your office wall, send a self-addressed, 9 X 12 envelope with two first-class stamps to:

Bookhome Publishing
"10 Commandments" Certificate
P.O. Box 5900
Navarre, FL 32566

I'd love to hear from you. Write and let me know how you are doing and what works best for your business. I would like to hear how you started your business, what hard times you have conquered, and how your business has changed you. Of course, I'd especially love to know which of the "10 Commandments" most helped you, and in what ways.

If you have any suggestions for how this book can be better in future editions, please pass them on. You can write me in care of the publisher at the above address, or e-mail me at margkirk@flash.net. Should that e-mail address change or be inoperative for any reason, simply visit www.bookhome.com and send an e-mail to the publisher, and it will get passed on to me.

Wishing you great success. Enjoy the journey.

Marguerite Kirk
January 1, 1999

Recommended Reading

General Business

Books

The 4 Routes to Entrepreneurial Success, John B. Miner (1996, Berrett-Koehler Publishing)

The 80/20 Principle: The Secret of Achieving More With Less, Richard Koch (1998, Bantam Doubleday Dell Publishing)

Adams Streetwise Small Business Start-Up: Your Comprehensive Guide to Starting and Managing a Business, Bob Adams (1996, Adams Publishing)

Business Start-Up Guide, Tom Severance (1998, Tycoon Publishing)

Do What You Love, the Money Will Follow: Discovering Your Right Livelihood, Marsha Sinetar (1989, DTP)

Entrepreneurs Are Made, Not Born, Lloyd E. Shefsky (1996, McGraw-Hill)

How to Succeed in Business by Breaking All the Rules: A Plan for Entrepreneurs, Dan S. Kennedy and Scott DeGarmo (1997, E. P. Dutton)

Making a Living Without a Job: Winning Ways for Creating Work That You Love, Barbara J. Winter (1993, Bantam Doubleday Dell Publishing)

Smart Choices: A Practical Guide to Making Better Decisions, John S. Hammond, Ralph L. Keeney, Howard Raiffa (1998, Harvard Business School Press)

Organizations

American Business Women's Association, 9100 Ward Parkway, P. O. Box 8728, Kansas City, MO 64114-0728, Phone: (816) 361-6621, Fax: (816) 361-4991, Website: www.abwahq.org

National Association of Female Executives, Phone (800) 634-6233, Website: www.nafe. com

National Association of Women Business Owners, 1100 Wayne Ave., Suite 830, Silver Spring, MD 20910, Phone: (301) 608-2590, Fax: (301) 608-2596, Website: www. nawbo.org

Business Plans and Marketing

Books

301 Do-It-Yourself Marketing Ideas: From America's Most Innovative Small Companies, Sam Decker, Editor (1997, Inc. Publishing)

301 Great Customer Service Ideas: From America's Most Innovative Small Companies, Nancy Artz, Editor (1998, Inc. Publishing)

1001 Ways to Market Yourself and Your Small Business, Lisa Angowski Rogak Shaw (1997, Perigee)

Customers for Life, Carl Sewell (1998, Pocket Books)

Guerrilla Marketing: Secrets for Making Big Profits from Your Small Business, Jay Conrad Levinson (1984, Houghton Mifflin Co.)

How to Write a Business Plan, Mike McKeever (1992, Nolo Press)

Marketing Without Megabucks: How to Sell Anything on a Shoestring, Shel Horowitz (1993, Simon & Schuster)

The Perfect Business Plan Made Simple, William Lasher (1994, Made Simple)

Magazines

American Demographics, Published by Cowles Business Media, Phone: (607) 273-6343, Website: www. demographics. com

Business Lifestyle

Books

The Home Team: How to Live, Love and Work at Home, Scott Gregory and Shirley Siluk Gregory (1999, Bookhome Publishing)

Honey, I Want to Start My Own Business: A Planning Guide for Couples, Azriela Jaffe (1996, HarperBusiness)

How to Raise a Family and a Career Under One Roof: A Parent's Guide to Home Business, Lisa M. Roberts (1997, Bookhaven Press)

In Love and In Business: How Entrepreneurial Couples are Changing the Rules of Business and Marriage, Sharon Nelton (1986, John Wiley & Sons Inc.)

Magazines

The Home Team™ Online work-at-home magazine, Published by Bookhome Publishing, Website: www. bookhome.com

Other Resources

Home-Based Working Moms, P.O. Box 500164, Austin, TX 78750, Website: www.hbwm.com

The Entrepreneurial Parent, Website: www.en-parent.com

Small Business and Home Business

Books

201 Great Ideas for Your Small Business, introduction by Jane Applegate (1998, Bloomberg Press)

Employ Your PC: Businesses That Can be Run From Home, Gabriele Massie (1996, Red Tail Publishing)

Homemade Money, Barbara Brabec (1997, Betterway Books)

How to Build a Successful One-Person Business, Veltisezar B. Bautista (1995, Bookhaus Publishers)

Recommended Reading

Working from Home: Everything You Need to Know About Living and Working Under the Same Roof, Paul and Sarah Edwards (1994, Tarcher/Putnam)

Working Solo: The Real Guide to Freedom & Financial Success with Your Own Business, Terri Lonier (1994, Portico Press)

Magazines

Entrepreneur, Published monthly by Entrepreneur Media Inc., Phone: (800) 274-6229, Website: www.entrepreneurmag. com

Home Business News, Published quarterly by the American Home Business Association, Phone: (801) 273-5450, Website: www.homebusiness.com

Home Office Computing, Published monthly by Scholastic Inc., Phone: (800) 288-7812, Website: www. smalloffice.com

Income Opportunities, Published monthly by IO Publications Inc., Website: www.incomeops.com

Organizations

American Association of Home-Based Businesses Inc., Beverley Williams, President, P.O. Box 10023, Rockville, MD 20849, Phone: (800) 447-9710, (301) 963-9153, Fax: (301) 963-7042, Website: www. aahbb.org

American Home Business Association, Larry Brockman, President, 4505 S. Wasatch Blvd., Salt Lake City, UT 84124, Phone: (800) 664-2422. Website: www. homebusiness.com

Home Office Association of America, Richard Ekstrakt, Chairman, 909 Third Ave., Suite 990, New York, NY 10002-4731, Phone: (800) 809-4622, (212) 980-4622 , Website: www.hoaa.com

National Association of Home-Based Businesses, Rudolph Lewis, President, 10451 Mill Run Circle, Suite 400, Owings Mills, MD 21117, Phone: (410) 363-3698, Website: www.usahomebusiness.com

National Association for the Self-Employed, Bennie Thayer, President, P. O. Box 34116, Washington, D.C. 34116, Phone: (800) 232-6273, (202) 466-2100, Website: www. nase.org

National Federation of Independent Business, Jack Faris, President, 53 Century Blvd., Suite 300, Nashville, TN 37214, Phone: (800) NFIB-NOW, (615) 872-5300

(For information on other organizations in your area, contact your local or state chamber of commerce or small-business development center. Or call SCORE–the Service Corps of Retired Executives, a resource partner of the U.S. Small Business Administration–at (800) 634-0245.)

Other Resources
CompuServe, Working at Home Forum, Keyword: go work

Small Business Advancement National Center, Website: www.sbaer.uca.edu

U. S. Small Business Administration, Phone: (800) 8-ASK-SBA, Website: www.sbaonline.sba.gov

Taxes, Finances and Law

Books
The American Bar Association Guide to Workplace Law: Everything You Need to Know About Your Rights As an Employee or Employer, Barbara J. Fick, the American Bar Association (1997, Times Books)

Don't Let the IRS Destroy Your Small Business: Seventy-Six Mistakes to Avoid, Michael Savage (1998, Perseus Press)

The Entrepreneur's Guide to Business Law, Constance E. Bagley and Craig E. Dauchy (1997, International Thomson Publishing)

Hiring Independent Contractors: The Employers' Legal Guide, Stephen Fishman (1997, Nolo Press)

Insuring the Bottom Line: How to Protect Your Company from Liabilities, Catastrophes and Other Business Risks, David Russell (1996, Silver Lake Publishing)

The Legal Guide for Starting & Running a Small Business, Fred S. Steingold (1998, Nolo Press)

Money-Smart Secrets for the Self-Employed, Linda Stern (1997, Random House)

Stand Up to the IRS, Frederick Daily (1999, Nolo Press)

The Trick to Money is Having Some, Stuart Wilde (1995, Hay House Inc.)

Other Resources
Internal Revenue Service, Website: www.irs.ustreas.gov. Recommended publications include the Tax Guide for Small Business (publication 334), Business Use of Your Home (publication 587) and Self-Employment Tax (publication 533).

Nolo Press' Self-Help Law Center, Website: www.nolo.com. Includes information on writing and negotiating contracts, as well as other legal necessities for small and home-based businesses.

Intuition and Motivation

Books
Aha!: 10 Ways to Free Your Creative Spirit and Find Your Great Ideas, Jordan E. Ayan (1997, Crown Publishing)

Answers from Within, William J. Byron (1998, Macmillan)

Care of the Soul, Thomas Moore (1994, Harperperennial Library)

Creating Money, Sanaya Roman and Duane Packer (1988, H.J. Kramer)

Don't Sweat the Small Stuff at Work: Simple Ways to Minimize Stress and Conflict While Bringing Out the Best in Yourself and Others, Richard Carlson (1998, Hyperion)

First Things First, Stephen R. Covey (1996, Fireside)

How to Win Friends and Influence People, Dale Carnegie (Pocket Books)

The Magic of Thinking Big, David J. Schwartz (Prentice-Hall Inc.)

Practical Intuition for Success: A Step-By-Step Program to Increase Your Wealth Today, Laura Day and Martin Edelson (1997, Harpercollins)

Sanctuaries, Jack and Marcia Kelly (1996, Bell Tower)

The Seven Spiritual Laws of Success: A Practical Guide to the Fulfillment of Your Dreams, Deepak Chopra (1995, Amber-Allen Publishing)

Think and Grow Rich, Napoleon Hill (1996, Ballantine Books)

Visionary Business: An Entrepreneur's Guide to Success, Marc Allen (1995, New World Library)

Wishcraft: How to Get What You Really Want, Barbara Sher and Annie Gottlieb (1986, Ballantine Books)

Your Life's Work, Tami Coyne (1998, Berkley Publishing Group)

Other Resources

Developing Intuition, Shakti Gawain (1991, VHS tape)

Index

About the Author

Marguerite Kirk graduated from the University of Georgia Law School with an undergraduate double major in journalism and business. She began practicing with the law firm of the then-Governor of Georgia Carl Sanders, and was the first female attorney ever to practice in Augusta, Georgia. With more than 25 years' experience, specializing in business law and small business reorganization, Kirk has become recognized as one of the top experts in her field. She has often been consulted by and quoted as a knowledgeable business attorney by the Associated Press, *Fort Worth Star Telegram*, *PC Magazine* and *Dallas Magazine*. She also has appeared on radio and television talk shows in Texas, Florida, California and New York. Kirk also is the author of *Holding Onto the American Dream: How Small Businesses Can Conquer Financial Difficulties*. She lives in the Dallas/Ft. Worth area.

Also from Bookhome

The Home Team: How to Live, Love & Work at Home

Forget the traditional choices of the work world, where it can be all or nothing: your career or your family. *The Home Team* shows husbands and wives how to enjoy the best of both worlds by working at home in the same or separate businesses. Authors Scott Gregory and Shirley Siluk Gregory combine real-life stories, advice and humor to show how and why to create a successful work-at-home partnership–known as a Home Team–or make an existing one more enjoyable.

Packed with solid information, this book tackles such topics as how couples with wildly different personalities can work in the same home successfully; how to savor the joys of Home Team parenting, yet get your work done; how to ignite the flames of romance–before, during and after work; and potential career benefits for both men and women.

Other Bookhome Products

In addition to its books, Bookhome also publishes many special reports targeting specific needs of small-business owners, writers and others looking to live and work better. Titles include:

> *100 Steps to Home Team Success: A Business Plan Guide*
> *for Work-at-Home Couples*
> *101 Ways to Beat Writer's Block*
> *How to Write a Book: 101 Tips for Authors*
> *99 Steps to Writing Success: What Every Writer Should Know*
> *About the Word Business*
> *Understanding Copyright: A Guide for Writers*

To order any of these reports, call Bookhome toll-free at 1-877-326-6546 (877-3-BOOKHOME) or 1-877-232-2438 (877-BEACHFUN), visit http://www.bookhome.com or fax your order, with name, address, phone number and credit card information, to 850-939-4953. Fax and online ordering available 24 hours a day, seven days a week. Reports are $6.95 each, with $1 shipping per report. Please specify titles and number of copies desired. Florida residents, please add 6.50 % sales tax.

Order Form

• If you would like copies of *10 Commandments of Small-Business Success* for yourself or for a friend, visit your favorite bookstore or call Bookhome Publishing toll free during business hours at:

1-877-326-6546 (877-3-BOOKHOME)
1-877-232-2438 (877-BEACHFUN)

Please have your Visa, MasterCard or American Express card handy. Only orders and questions about orders at this number, please. Direct other questions to 850-936-4050. Your satisfaction is guaranteed.

• You can find more information about *10 Commandments of Small-Business Success* and other Bookhome books and reports, as well as order them safely 24 hours a day by visiting our website:

http://www.bookhome.com

• You also can order at your convenience by completing the form below and faxing it to us at: 850-939-4953.

• Or you can order by mail by copying or removing this form and sending it with a check or credit card information to: Bookhome Publishing, P.O. Box 5900, Navarre, FL 32566.

Please send me   copies of *10 Commandments of Small-Business Success* in softcover at $14.95 each.

Please send me   copies of *The Home Team* in hardcover at $22.95 each.

Please send me   copies of *The Home Team* in softcover at $14.95 each.

Name:

Address:

City/State/Zip:

Telephone and E-mail:

Shipping: $4 for first book via Priority Mail, $2 for each additional book. Florida residents, please add 6.50% sales tax.

Credit card number:
Type of card: Expiration date: /
Name on card:

Signature:

Order Form

• If you would like copies of *10 Commandments of Small-Business Success* for yourself or for a friend, visit your favorite bookstore or call Bookhome Publishing toll free during business hours at:

1-877-326-6546 (877-3-BOOKHOME)
1-877-232-2438 (877-BEACHFUN)

Please have your Visa, MasterCard or American Express card handy. Only orders and questions about orders at this number, please. Direct other questions to 850-936-4050. Your satisfaction is guaranteed.

• You can find more information about *10 Commandments of Small-Business Success* and other Bookhome books and reports, as well as order them safely 24 hours a day by visiting our website:

http://www.bookhome.com

• You also can order at your convenience by completing the form below and faxing it to us at: 850-939-4953.

• Or you can order by mail by copying or removing this form and sending it with a check or credit card information to: Bookhome Publishing, P.O. Box 5900, Navarre, FL 32566.

Please send me ____ copies of *10 Commandments of Small-Business Success* in softcover at $14.95 each.

Please send me ____ copies of *The Home Team* in hardcover at $22.95 each.

Please send me ____ copies of *The Home Team* in softcover at $14.95 each.

Name:

Address:

City/State/Zip:

Telephone and E-mail:

Shipping: $4 for first book via Priority Mail, $2 for each additional book. Florida residents, please add 6.50% sales tax.

Credit card number:
Type of card: Expiration date: /
Name on card:

Signature: